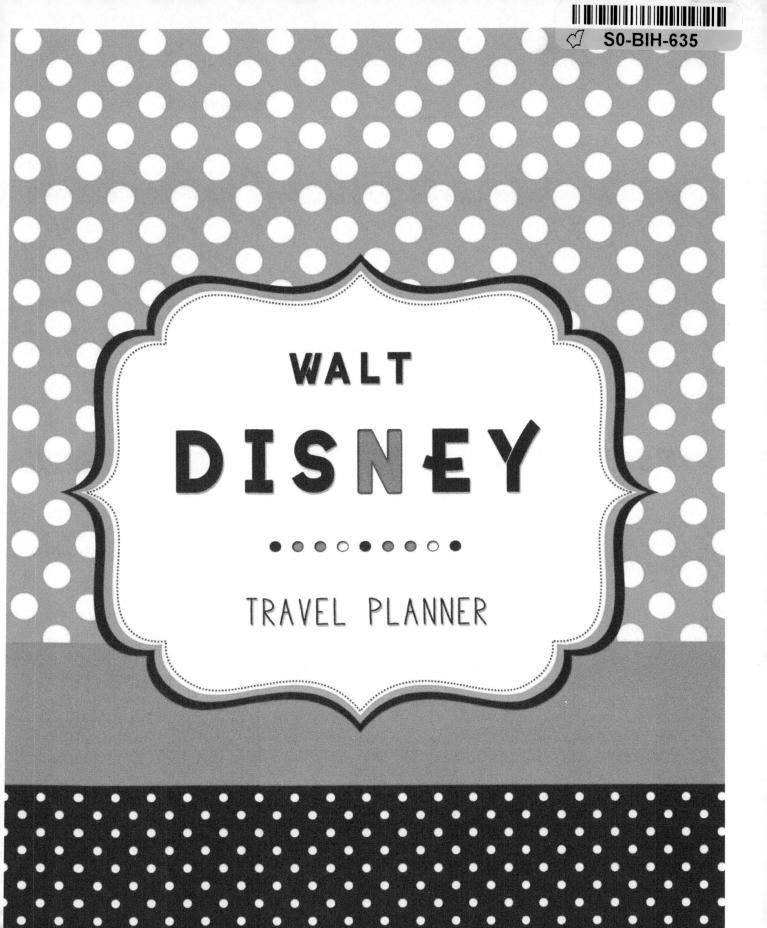

WALT

DISNEY

● ● ● ○ ● ● ● ○ ●

TRAVEL PLANNER

TRAVEL Details

TRIP DATES: ___/___/___ TO ___/___/___   NUMBER OF NIGHTS: _____

TRAVEL PLANNING

Travel Agency: _____   Website: _____

Agent: _____   Log In: _____   Password: _____

Phone: _____   Confirmation: _____

TRANSFER TO/FROM AIRPORT: | AIRPORT PARKING

Date	Service	Time	Reservation #	Lot	Location

FLIGHTS OVERVIEW

Airline: _____   Phone #: _____   Frequent Flyer #: _____

Date	Depart from	Time	Confirmation	Flight #	Arrive at

CAR RENTAL/MAGIC EXPRESS

Company: _____   Phone: _____   Rewards : _____

Date	Pick-up Location	Time	Drop-off Location	Time	Confirmation :

ACCOMMODATIONS

Hotel: _____   Address: _____   Phone: _____

Date: _____ Check In Time: _____ Room: _____ Check Out Time: _____ Confirmation: _____

Hotel: _____   Address: _____   Phone: _____

Date: _____ Check In Time: _____ Room: _____ Check Out Time: _____ Confirmation: _____

PLANNING Timeline

NOTES

- Establish a budget and start a savings fund
- Create an account on MyDisneyExperience.com
- Begin your research
  - Resorts: on-site or off-site
  - Special offers/Vacation packages
  - Disney Dining Plans
  - Attendance calendars for best time to visit
  - Restaurants, tours and extra experiences
- Make your Disney Vacation Bucket List

8-10 MONTHS BEFORE - *NOTHING'S IMPOSSIBLE. ~THE DOORKNOB*

- Select your travel dates
- Book chosen hotel/resort
- Make a list of your most wanted reservations

6-8 MONTHS BEFORE - *ALL IT TAKES IS FAITH & TRUST. ~PETER PAN*

- Decide on number of days you will spend at each park
- Check park hours for you trip and designate park days
- For each day/park, write down what activities you'll be doing
- Make a list of possible *FastPass* attractions
- Pick dining options - 1st choice, 2nd choice, & 3rd choice
- Purchase park tickets and link to MyDisneyExperience.com

180 DAYS BEFORE - *GIVING UP IS FOR ROOKIES. ~PHILOCTETES*

- On-Site Guests: You can make all of your reservations today!
- Off-Site Guests: You'll need to log in each day to make reservations
- Book air travel

PLANNING Timeline

60 DAYS BEFORE - *HAKUNA MATATA. ~TIMONE & PUMBA*

- On-Site Guests: FastPass+ reservations opens to the entire length of your stay
- Move from **Basic Itinerary** to **Touring Plan!**
- Customize your Magic Band
- Start a walking regimen
- Make Magical Express reservations or other transportation arrangements

30 DAYS BEFORE - *TO INFINITY AND BEYOND! ~BUZZ LIGHTYEAR*

- Off-Site Guests: FastPass+ reservations open. Must schedule day by day
- Confirm park hours and review your Touring Plan
- Watch YouTube videos of attractions your children are unsure of
- Print a packing list and check your closet for needed items
- Display your Disney count-down calendar

2 WEEKS BEFORE- *MOST EVERYONE'S MAD HERE. ~ CHESHIRE CAT*

- Purchase needed clothing, toiletries and other travel necessities
- Start packing
- Stop mail/newspaper for you vacation
- Complete the "While We're Away for house sitter/neighbors/family

1 WEEK BEFORE - *JUST KEEP SWIMMING. ~DORY*

- Confirm reservations
- Refill prescriptions
- Review packing checklist and purchase needed items

THE DAY BEFORE - *LET IT GO! ~ELSA*

- Check into your airline
- Finish Disney resort online check-in
- Finish packing, weigh your luggage
- Charge tech gadgets

ON THE WAY OUT - *THERE'S THE WHOLE WORLD AT YOUR FEET. ~BERT*

- Unplug/turn off appliances
- Empty trash
- Set security system

VACATION Budget

		Budget	Actual Cost	Notes
TRANSPORTATION	Airfare (+ baggage fees)			
	Airport Parking			
	Bus/Taxi/Shuttle/Subway			
	Car Rental			
	Gasoline			
	Tolls & Other Fees			
	Subtotal			
LODGING	Hotel/Motel/Campsite			
	Taxes & Fees			
	Parking/Valet			
	Hotel Service Tips			
	Subtotal			
FOOD & DRINK	Disney Dining Plan			
	Table Service Meals			
	Quick/Counter Service Meals			
	Snacks & Drinks			
	Groceries			
	Other			
	Subtotal			
TICKETS	Park Tickets			
	Special Experiences			
	Park Tours			
	Sports and Recreation			
	Subtotal			
OTHER	Passports/Visas			
	Travelers Insurance			
	Clothes/Accessories			
	Travel Supplies			
	Luggage			
	Souvenirs/Gifts			
	Subtotal			

TOTAL BUDGET	TOTAL EXPENSES	DIFFERENCE

VACATION Budget

		Budget	Actual Cost	Notes
TRANSPORTATION	Airfare (+ baggage fees)			
	Airport Parking			
	Bus/Taxi/Shuttle/Subway			
	Car Rental			
	Gasoline			
	Tolls & Other Fees			
	Subtotal			
LODGING	Hotel/Motel/Campsite			
	Taxes & Fees			
	Parking/Valet			
	Hotel Service Tips			
	Subtotal			
FOOD & DRINK	Disney Dining Plan			
	Table Service Meals			
	Quick/Counter Service Meals			
	Snacks & Drinks			
	Groceries			
	Other			
	Subtotal			
TICKETS	Park Tickets			
	Special Experiences			
	Park Tours			
	Sports and Recreation			
	Subtotal			
OTHER	Passports/Visas			
	Travelers Insurance			
	Clothes/Accessories			
	Travel Supplies			
	Luggage			
	Souvenirs/Gifts			
	Subtotal			

TOTAL BUDGET	TOTAL EXPENSES	DIFFERENCE

VACATION Budget

	Budget	Actual Cost	Notes
TRANSPORTATION			
Airfare (+ baggage fees)			
Airport Parking			
Bus/Taxi/Shuttle/Subway			
Car Rental			
Gasoline			
Tolls & Other Fees			
Subtotal			
LODGING			
Hotel/Motel/Campsite			
Taxes & Fees			
Parking/Valet			
Hotel Service Tips			
Subtotal			
FOOD & DRINK			
Disney Dining Plan			
Table Service Meals			
Quick/Counter Service Meals			
Snacks & Drinks			
Groceries			
Other			
Subtotal			
TICKETS			
Park Tickets			
Special Experiences			
Park Tours			
Sports and Recreation			
Subtotal			
OTHER			
Passports/Visas			
Travelers Insurance			
Clothes/Accessories			
Travel Supplies			
Luggage			
Souvenirs/Gifts			
Subtotal			

TOTAL BUDGET	TOTAL EXPENSES	DIFFERENCE

CHOOSE Accommodations

DISNEY RESORT VS. OFF-SITE	
Disney Resort	Off-Site
Cost:	Cost:
Transportation:	Transportation:
Amenities:	Amenities:
Other:	Other:

HOTEL/RESORT: _____ **RATING:** _____

Location: _____ **Check-in:** _____ **Check-out:** _____

Amenities:

Nearby Attractions:

- ☐ Free breakfast
- ☐ Restaurant
- ☐ Free Wi-Fi
- ☐ Free parking
- ☐ Room service
- ☐ Fitness center

- ☐ Swimming pool
- ☐ Smoke free
- ☐ Pet Friendly
- ☐ _____
- ☐ _____
- ☐ _____

Room Type: _____ **$/Night:** _____

Discount/Deals:

Cancellation Policy:

HOTEL/RESORT: _____ **RATING:** _____

Location: _____ **Check-in:** _____ **Check-out:** _____

Amenities:

Nearby Attractions:

- ☐ Free breakfast
- ☐ Restaurant
- ☐ Free Wi-Fi
- ☐ Free parking
- ☐ Room service
- ☐ Fitness center

- ☐ Swimming pool
- ☐ Smoke free
- ☐ Pet Friendly
- ☐ _____
- ☐ _____
- ☐ _____

Room Type: _____ **$/Night:** _____

Discount/Deals:

Cancellation Policy:

CHOOSE Accommodations

DISNEY RESORT VS. OFF-SITE	
Disney Resort	Off-Site
Cost:	Cost:
Transportation:	Transportation:
Amenities:	Amenities:
Other:	Other:

HOTEL/RESORT: **RATING:**

Location: **Check-in:**   **Check-out:**

Amenities: **Nearby Attractions:**

☐ Free breakfast   ☐ Swimming pool

☐ Restaurant   ☐ Smoke free

☐ Free Wi-Fi   ☐ Pet Friendly

☐ Free parking   ☐ _____

☐ Room service   ☐ _____

☐ Fitness center   ☐ _____

Room Type: **$/Night:**

Discount/Deals:

Cancellation Policy:

HOTEL/RESORT: **RATING:**

Location: **Check-in:**   **Check-out:**

Amenities: **Nearby Attractions:**

☐ Free breakfast   ☐ Swimming pool

☐ Restaurant   ☐ Smoke free

☐ Free Wi-Fi   ☐ Pet Friendly

☐ Free parking   ☐ _____

☐ Room service   ☐ _____

☐ Fitness center   ☐ _____

Room Type: **$/Night:**

Discount/Deals:

Cancellation Policy:

CHOOSE Accommodations

DISNEY RESORT VS. OFF-SITE	
Disney Resort	Off-Site
Cost:	Cost:
Transportation:	Transportation:
Amenities:	Amenities:
Other:	Other:

HOTEL/RESORT: _____ **RATING:** ____

Location: **Check-in:**   **Check-out:**

Amenities: **Nearby Attractions:**

☐ Free breakfast   ☐ Swimming pool

☐ Restaurant   ☐ Smoke free

☐ Free Wi-Fi   ☐ Pet Friendly

☐ Free parking   ☐ _____

☐ Room service   ☐ _____

☐ Fitness center   ☐ _____

Room Type: *$/Night:*

Discount/Deals:

Cancellation Policy:

HOTEL/RESORT: _____ **RATING:** ____

Location: **Check-in:**   **Check-out:**

Amenities: **Nearby Attractions:**

☐ Free breakfast   ☐ Swimming pool

☐ Restaurant   ☐ Smoke free

☐ Free Wi-Fi   ☐ Pet Friendly

☐ Free parking   ☐ _____

☐ Room service   ☐ _____

☐ Fitness center   ☐ _____

Room Type: *$/Night:*

Discount/Deals:

Cancellation Policy:

CHOOSE an Offer

PACKAGE/OFFER:

Resort :   **Room Type:**   **Discount:**

 # Days/Nights: **Check in Date:**   **Check out Date:**

Tickets	Dining Plan	Details:
☐ Base	☐ Quick Service	
☐ Park Hopper	☐ Standard	**Restrictions:**
☐ Water Park Fun & More	☐ Deluxe	
☐ No Expiration	☐ Premium	

Cost: $

PACKAGE/OFFER:

Resort :   **Room Type:**   **Discount:**

 # Days/Nights: **Check in Date:**   **Check out Date:**

Tickets	Dining Plan	Details:
☐ Base	☐ Quick Service	
☐ Park Hopper	☐ Standard	**Restrictions:**
☐ Water Park Fun & More	☐ Deluxe	
☐ No Expiration	☐ Premium	

Cost: $

PACKAGE/OFFER:

Resort :   **Room Type:**   **Discount:**

 # Days/Nights: **Check in Date:**   **Check out Date:**

Tickets	Dining Plan	Details:
☐ Base	☐ Quick Service	
☐ Park Hopper	☐ Standard	**Restrictions:**
☐ Water Park Fun & More	☐ Deluxe	
☐ No Expiration	☐ Premium	

Cost: $

CHOOSE an Offer

PACKAGE/OFFER:

Resort :   Room Type: Discount:

Days/Nights: Check in Date: Check out Date:

Tickets	Dining Plan	Details:
☐ Base	☐ Quick Service	
☐ Park Hopper	☐ Standard	Restrictions:
☐ Water Park Fun & More	☐ Deluxe	
☐ No Expiration	☐ Premium	

Cost: $

PACKAGE/OFFER:

Resort :   Room Type: Discount:

Days/Nights: Check in Date: Check out Date:

Tickets	Dining Plan	Details:
☐ Base	☐ Quick Service	
☐ Park Hopper	☐ Standard	Restrictions:
☐ Water Park Fun & More	☐ Deluxe	
☐ No Expiration	☐ Premium	

Cost: $

PACKAGE/OFFER:

Resort :   Room Type: Discount:

Days/Nights: Check in Date: Check out Date:

Tickets	Dining Plan	Details:
☐ Base	☐ Quick Service	
☐ Park Hopper	☐ Standard	Restrictions:
☐ Water Park Fun & More	☐ Deluxe	
☐ No Expiration	☐ Premium	

Cost: $

CHOOSE an Offer

PACKAGE/OFFER:

Resort :   **Room Type:**   **Discount:**

 # Days/Nights: **Check in Date:**   **Check out Date:**

Tickets   **Dining Plan**   **Details:**

☐ Base   ☐ Quick Service

☐ Park Hopper   ☐ Standard   **Restrictions:**

☐ Water Park Fun & More   ☐ Deluxe

☐ No Expiration   ☐ Premium

                                                            Cost: ☐ $

PACKAGE/OFFER:

Resort :   **Room Type:**   **Discount:**

 # Days/Nights: **Check in Date:**   **Check out Date:**

Tickets   **Dining Plan**   **Details:**

☐ Base   ☐ Quick Service

☐ Park Hopper   ☐ Standard   **Restrictions:**

☐ Water Park Fun & More   ☐ Deluxe

☐ No Expiration   ☐ Premium

                                                            Cost: ☐ $

PACKAGE/OFFER:

Resort :   **Room Type:**   **Discount:**

 # Days/Nights: **Check in Date:**   **Check out Date:**

Tickets   **Dining Plan**   **Details:**

☐ Base   ☐ Quick Service

☐ Park Hopper   ☐ Standard   **Restrictions:**

☐ Water Park Fun & More   ☐ Deluxe

☐ No Expiration   ☐ Premium

                                                            Cost: ☐ $

CHOOSE Transportation

DRIVING VS. FLYING			
Driving Expenses		**Flying Expenses**	
Gas	$	Flight Tickets	$
Tolls	$	Baggage Fees	$
Hotels	$	Parking/Taxi Service	$
Meals on the Road	$	Tolls/Tips	$
Car Maintenance	$	Meals/Snacks	$
	$	Rental Car	$
TOTAL	$	*TOTAL*	$

AIRLINE:

FLIGHT #	DEPARTING FROM	TIME	ARRIVING AT	TIME	STOPS	$/PERSON

AIRLINE:

FLIGHT #	DEPARTING FROM	TIME	ARRIVING AT	TIME	STOPS	$/PERSON

AIRLINE:

FLIGHT #	DEPARTING FROM	TIME	ARRIVING AT	TIME	STOPS	$/PERSON

AIRLINE:

FLIGHT #	DEPARTING FROM	TIME	ARRIVING AT	TIME	STOPS	$/PERSON

CHOOSE Transportation

DRIVING VS. FLYING			
Driving Expenses		**Flying Expenses**	
Gas	$	Flight Tickets	$
Tolls	$	Baggage Fees	$
Hotels	$	Parking/Taxi Service	$
Meals on the Road	$	Tolls/Tips	$
Car Maintenance	$	Meals/Snacks	$
	$	Rental Car	$
TOTAL	$	*TOTAL*	$

AIRLINE:

FLIGHT #	DEPARTING FROM	TIME	ARRIVING AT	TIME	STOPS	$/PERSON

AIRLINE:

FLIGHT #	DEPARTING FROM	TIME	ARRIVING AT	TIME	STOPS	$/PERSON

AIRLINE:

FLIGHT #	DEPARTING FROM	TIME	ARRIVING AT	TIME	STOPS	$/PERSON

AIRLINE:

FLIGHT #	DEPARTING FROM	TIME	ARRIVING AT	TIME	STOPS	$/PERSON

CHOOSE Transportation

DRIVING VS. FLYING			
Driving Expenses		**Flying Expenses**	
Gas	$	Flight Tickets	$
Tolls	$	Baggage Fees	$
Hotels	$	Parking/Taxi Service	$
Meals on the Road	$	Tolls/Tips	$
Car Maintenance	$	Meals/Snacks	$
	$	Rental Car	$
TOTAL	$	*TOTAL*	$

AIRLINE:

FLIGHT #	DEPARTING FROM	TIME	ARRIVING AT	TIME	STOPS	$/PERSON

AIRLINE:

FLIGHT #	DEPARTING FROM	TIME	ARRIVING AT	TIME	STOPS	$/PERSON

AIRLINE:

FLIGHT #	DEPARTING FROM	TIME	ARRIVING AT	TIME	STOPS	$/PERSON

AIRLINE:

FLIGHT #	DEPARTING FROM	TIME	ARRIVING AT	TIME	STOPS	$/PERSON

HOUSE SITTER Notes

GARAGE CODE	SECURITY CODE	WI-FI PASSWORD
_____	_____	_____

HOUSE ADDRESS: **HOUSE PHONE:**

CONTACT INFORMATION

's Email:	Phone:
's Email:	Phone:
Neighbor:	Phone:
Family/Friend:	Phone:

ITINERARY   PET INFORMATION

ITINERARY	PET INFORMATION
We're staying at:	Name:
Phone:	Vet:
We're returning: Time:	Phone:
	Notes:

INSTRUCTIONS

DAY 1	DAY 2	DAY 3	DAY 4	DAY 5	DAY 6	DAY 7

HOUSE SITTER Notes

GARAGE CODE	SECURITY CODE	WI-FI PASSWORD
_____	_____	_____

HOUSE ADDRESS: **HOUSE PHONE:**

CONTACT INFORMATION

's Email:	Phone:
's Email:	Phone:
Neighbor:	Phone:
Family/Friend:	Phone:

ITINERARY

	PET INFORMATION
We're staying at:	Name:
Phone:	Vet:
We're returning: Time:	Phone:
	Notes:

INSTRUCTIONS

DAY 8	DAY 9	DAY 10	DAY 11	DAY 12	DAY 13	DAY 14

HOUSE SITTER Notes

GARAGE CODE	SECURITY CODE	WI-FI PASSWORD
_____	_____	_____

HOUSE ADDRESS: **HOUSE PHONE:**

CONTACT INFORMATION

's Email:	Phone:
's Email:	Phone:
Neighbor:	Phone:
Family/Friend:	Phone:

ITINERARY

We're staying at:	
Phone:	
We're returning: Time:	

PET INFORMATION

Name:
Vet:
Phone:
Notes:

INSTRUCTIONS

DAY 15	DAY 16	DAY 17	DAY 18	DAY 19	DAY 20	DAY 21

HOUSE SITTER Notes

HOUSE ADDRESS: **HOUSE PHONE:**

CONTACT INFORMATION

's Email:	Phone:
's Email:	Phone:
Neighbor:	Phone:
Family/Friend:	Phone:

ITINERARY

We're staying at:	
Phone:	
We're returning:	Time:

PET INFORMATION

Name:
Vet:
Phone:
Notes:

INSTRUCTIONS

DAY 22	DAY 23	DAY 24	DAY 25	DAY 26	DAY 27	DAY 28

HOUSE SITTER Notes

GARAGE CODE	SECURITY CODE	WI-FI PASSWORD
_____	_____	_____

HOUSE ADDRESS: _____ **HOUSE PHONE:** _____

CONTACT INFORMATION

's Email: _____	Phone: _____
's Email: _____	Phone: _____
Neighbor: _____	Phone: _____
Family/Friend: _____	Phone: _____

ITINERARY

We're staying at: _____

Phone: _____

We're returning: _____ Time: _____

PET INFORMATION

Name: _____

Vet: _____

Phone: _____

Notes: _____

INSTRUCTIONS

_____

_____

_____

_____

DAY 29	DAY 30	DAY 31	DAY 32	DAY 33	DAY 34	DAY 35

DISNEY WORLD Bucket List

	PARK/LOCATION	THINGS TO DO
1		
2		
3		
4		
5		
6		
7		
8		
9		
10		
11		
12		
13		
14		
15		
16		
17		
18		
19		
20		

DISNEY WORLD Bucket List

	PARK/LOCATION	THINGS TO DO
21		
22		
23		
24		
25		
26		
27		
28		
29		
30		
31		
32		
33		
34		
35		
36		
37		
38		
39		
40		

DISNEYWORLD Bucket List

	PARK/LOCATION	THINGS TO DO
41		
42		
43		
44		
45		
46		
47		
48		
49		
50		
51		
52		
53		
54		
55		
56		
57		
58		
59		
60		

DISNEY Activities

Magic Kingdom	# Days _____

- [ ]
- [ ]
- [ ]
- [ ]
- [ ]
- [ ]
- [ ]
- [ ]
- [ ]
- [ ]

RIDES	FP?	LOCATION
	[ ]	
	[ ]	
	[ ]	
	[ ]	
	[ ]	
	[ ]	
	[ ]	
	[ ]	
	[ ]	
	[ ]	

SHOWS	FP?	LOCATION
	[ ]	
	[ ]	
	[ ]	
	[ ]	
	[ ]	
	[ ]	
	[ ]	

CHARACTER EXPERIENCES

Character:

Times:

Location:

Character:

Times:

Location:

Character:

Times:

Location:

Character:

Times:

Location:

RESTAURANTS	ADR?	LOCATION
	[ ]	
	[ ]	
	[ ]	
	[ ]	
	[ ]	
	[ ]	
	[ ]	

TOURS & SPECIAL EVENTS

DISNEY Activities

Magic Kingdom   # Days _____

RIDES	FP?	LOCATION
	☐	
	☐	
	☐	
	☐	
	☐	
	☐	
	☐	
	☐	
	☐	
	☐	

SHOWS	FP?	LOCATION
	☐	
	☐	
	☐	
	☐	
	☐	
	☐	
	☐	

RESTAURANTS	ADR?	LOCATION
	☐	
	☐	
	☐	
	☐	
	☐	
	☐	
	☐	

TOP 10 MUST DO'S

☐
☐
☐
☐
☐
☐
☐
☐
☐
☐

CHARACTER EXPERIENCES

Character:

Times:

Location:

Character:

Times:

Location:

Character:

Times:

Location:

Character:

Times:

Location:

TOURS & SPECIAL EVENTS

DISNEY Activities

Magic Kingdom   # Days _____

RIDES	FP?	LOCATION
	☐	
	☐	
	☐	
	☐	
	☐	
	☐	
	☐	
	☐	
	☐	
	☐	

SHOWS	FP?	LOCATION
	☐	
	☐	
	☐	
	☐	
	☐	
	☐	
	☐	

RESTAURANTS	ADR?	LOCATION
	☐	
	☐	
	☐	
	☐	
	☐	
	☐	
	☐	
	☐	

TOP 10 MUST DO'S

- ☐
- ☐
- ☐
- ☐
- ☐
- ☐
- ☐
- ☐
- ☐
- ☐

CHARACTER EXPERIENCES

Character:

Times:

Location:

Character:

Times:

Location:

Character:

Times:

Location:

Character:

Times:

Location:

Character:

Times:

Location:

TOURS & SPECIAL EVENTS

DISNEY Activities

Hollywood Studios   # Days _____

RIDES	FP?	LOCATION
	☐	
	☐	
	☐	
	☐	
	☐	
	☐	
	☐	
	☐	
	☐	
	☐	

SHOWS	FP?	LOCATION
	☐	
	☐	
	☐	
	☐	
	☐	
	☐	

RESTAURANTS	ADR?	LOCATION
	☐	
	☐	
	☐	
	☐	
	☐	

TOP 10 MUST DO'S

☐
☐
☐
☐
☐
☐
☐
☐
☐
☐

CHARACTER EXPERIENCES

Character:

Times:

Location:

Character:

Times:

Location:

Character:

Times:

Location:

Character:

Times:

Location:

TOURS & SPECIAL EVENTS

DISNEY Activities

Hollywood Studios   # Days _____

RIDES	FP?	LOCATION
	☐	
	☐	
	☐	
	☐	
	☐	
	☐	
	☐	
	☐	
	☐	
	☐	

SHOWS	FP?	LOCATION
	☐	
	☐	
	☐	
	☐	
	☐	
	☐	
	☐	

RESTAURANTS	ADR?	LOCATION
	☐	
	☐	
	☐	
	☐	
	☐	
	☐	
	☐	

TOP 10 MUST DO'S

☐
☐
☐
☐
☐
☐
☐
☐
☐
☐

CHARACTER EXPERIENCES

Character:

Times:

Location:

Character:

Times:

Location:

Character:

Times:

Location:

Character:

Times:

Location:

TOURS & SPECIAL EVENTS

DISNEY Activities

Hollywood Studios   # Days _____

RIDES	FP?	LOCATION
	☐	
	☐	
	☐	
	☐	
	☐	
	☐	
	☐	
	☐	
	☐	
	☐	

SHOWS	FP?	LOCATION
	☐	
	☐	
	☐	
	☐	
	☐	
	☐	
	☐	

RESTAURANTS	ADR?	LOCATION
	☐	
	☐	
	☐	
	☐	
	☐	
	☐	
	☐	

TOP 10 MUST DO'S

☐
☐
☐
☐
☐
☐
☐
☐
☐
☐

CHARACTER EXPERIENCES

Character:

Times:

Location:

Character:

Times:

Location:

Character:

Times:

Location:

Character:

Times:

Location:

TOURS & SPECIAL EVENTS

DISNEY Activities

Animal Kingdom   # Days _____

RIDES	FP?	LOCATION
	☐	
	☐	
	☐	
	☐	
	☐	
	☐	
	☐	
	☐	
	☐	
	☐	

SHOWS	FP?	LOCATION
	☐	
	☐	
	☐	
	☐	
	☐	
	☐	
	☐	

RESTAURANTS	ADR?	LOCATION
	☐	
	☐	
	☐	
	☐	
	☐	
	☐	
	☐	

TOP 10 MUST DO'S

☐
☐
☐
☐
☐
☐
☐
☐
☐
☐

CHARACTER EXPERIENCES

Character:
Times:
Location:
Character:
Times:
Location:
Character:
Times:
Location:
Character:
Times:
Location:

TOURS & SPECIAL EVENTS

DISNEY Activities

Animal Kingdom   # Days _____

RIDES	FP?	LOCATION
	☐	
	☐	
	☐	
	☐	
	☐	
	☐	
	☐	
	☐	
	☐	
	☐	

SHOWS	FP?	LOCATION
	☐	
	☐	
	☐	
	☐	
	☐	
	☐	
	☐	

RESTAURANTS	ADR?	LOCATION
	☐	
	☐	
	☐	
	☐	
	☐	
	☐	

TOP 10 MUST DO'S

☐
☐
☐
☐
☐
☐
☐
☐
☐
☐

CHARACTER EXPERIENCES

Character:

Times:

Location:

Character:

Times:

Location:

Character:

Times:

Location:

Character:

Times:

Location:

TOURS & SPECIAL EVENTS

DISNEY Activities

Animal Kingdom   # Days _____

RIDES	FP?	LOCATION
	☐	
	☐	
	☐	
	☐	
	☐	
	☐	
	☐	
	☐	
	☐	
	☐	

SHOWS	FP?	LOCATION
	☐	
	☐	
	☐	
	☐	
	☐	
	☐	
	☐	

RESTAURANTS	ADR?	LOCATION
	☐	
	☐	
	☐	
	☐	
	☐	
	☐	
	☐	
	☐	

TOP 10 MUST DO'S

☐
☐
☐
☐
☐
☐
☐
☐
☐
☐

CHARACTER EXPERIENCES

Character:
Times:
Location:
Character:
Times:
Location:
Character:
Times:
Location:
Character:
Times:
Location:

TOURS & SPECIAL EVENTS

DISNEY Activities

Epcot	# Days _____

RIDES	FP?	LOCATION
	☐	
	☐	
	☐	
	☐	
	☐	
	☐	
	☐	
	☐	
	☐	
	☐	

SHOWS	FP?	LOCATION
	☐	
	☐	
	☐	
	☐	
	☐	
	☐	
	☐	

RESTAURANTS	ADR?	LOCATION
	☐	
	☐	
	☐	
	☐	
	☐	
	☐	
	☐	

TOP 10 MUST DO'S

- ☐
- ☐
- ☐
- ☐
- ☐
- ☐
- ☐
- ☐
- ☐
- ☐

CHARACTER EXPERIENCES

Character:

Times:

Location:

Character:

Times:

Location:

Character:

Times:

Location:

Character:

Times:

Location:

TOURS & SPECIAL EVENTS

DISNEY Activities

Epcot   # Days _____

RIDES	FP?	LOCATION
	☐	
	☐	
	☐	
	☐	
	☐	
	☐	
	☐	
	☐	
	☐	
	☐	

SHOWS	FP?	LOCATION
	☐	
	☐	
	☐	
	☐	
	☐	
	☐	
	☐	

RESTAURANTS	ADR?	LOCATION
	☐	
	☐	
	☐	
	☐	
	☐	
	☐	
	☐	

TOP 10 MUST DO'S

- ☐
- ☐
- ☐
- ☐
- ☐
- ☐
- ☐
- ☐
- ☐
- ☐

CHARACTER EXPERIENCES

Character:

Times:

Location:

Character:

Times:

Location:

Character:

Times:

Location:

Character:

Times:

Location:

TOURS & SPECIAL EVENTS

DISNEY Activities

Epcot   # Days _____

RIDES	FP?	LOCATION
	☐	
	☐	
	☐	
	☐	
	☐	
	☐	
	☐	
	☐	
	☐	
	☐	

SHOWS	FP?	LOCATION
	☐	
	☐	
	☐	
	☐	
	☐	
	☐	
	☐	

RESTAURANTS	ADR?	LOCATION
	☐	
	☐	
	☐	
	☐	
	☐	
	☐	

TOP 10 MUST DO'S

☐
☐
☐
☐
☐
☐
☐
☐
☐
☐

CHARACTER EXPERIENCES

Character:
Times:
Location:
Character:
Times:
Location:
Character:
Times:
Location:
Character:
Times:
Location:

TOURS & SPECIAL EVENTS

DISNEY Activities

Disney Springs

SHOPPING	LOCATION

RESTAURANTS	ADR?	LOCATION
	☐	
	☐	
	☐	
	☐	
	☐	
	☐	
	☐	
	☐	
	☐	
	☐	
	☐	

TOP 10 MUST DO'S

☐
☐
☐
☐
☐
☐
☐
☐
☐
☐

ENTERTAINMENT

Date/Time:

Location:

Date/Time:

Location:

Date/Time:

Location:

Date/Time:

Location:

ACTIVITIES

DISNEY Activities

Disney Springs

	SHOPPING	LOCATION

RESTAURANTS	ADR?	LOCATION

TOP 10 MUST DO'S

- [ ]
- [ ]
- [ ]
- [ ]
- [ ]
- [ ]
- [ ]
- [ ]
- [ ]
- [ ]

ENTERTAINMENT

Date/Time:

Location:

Date/Time:

Location:

Date/Time:

Location:

Date/Time:

Location:

ACTIVITIES

DISNEY Activities

Disney Springs

SHOPPING	LOCATION

RESTAURANTS	ADR?	LOCATION
	☐	
	☐	
	☐	
	☐	
	☐	
	☐	
	☐	
	☐	
	☐	
	☐	
	☐	

TOP 10 MUST DO'S

☐
☐
☐
☐
☐
☐
☐
☐
☐
☐

ENTERTAINMENT

Date/Time:

Location:

Date/Time:

Location:

Date/Time:

Location:

Date/Time:

Location:

ACTIVITIES

TOURING Planner

DAY: ___/___	DAY: ___/___	DAY: ___/___	DAY: ___/___
PARK:	PARK:	PARK:	PARK:
to EMH: am/pm	to EMH: am/pm	to EMH: am/pm	to EMH: am/pm
Crowd Level:	Crowd Level:	Crowd Level:	Crowd Level:

RIDES

☐ FP+	☐ FP+	☐ FP+	☐ FP+
☐ FP+	☐ FP+	☐ FP+	☐ FP+
☐ FP+	☐ FP+	☐ FP+	☐ FP+
☐ FP+	☐ FP+	☐ FP+	☐ FP+
☐ FP+	☐ FP+	☐ FP+	☐ FP+

SHOWS/PARADES

☐ FP+	☐ FP+	☐ FP+	☐ FP+
☐ FP+	☐ FP+	☐ FP+	☐ FP+
☐ FP+	☐ FP+	☐ FP+	☐ FP+

CHARACTER EXPERIENCE

☐ FP+	☐ FP+	☐ FP+	☐ FP+
☐ FP+	☐ FP+	☐ FP+	☐ FP+

DINING

☐ ADR	☐ ADR	☐ ADR	☐ ADR
☐ ADR	☐ ADR	☐ ADR	☐ ADR
☐ ADR	☐ ADR	☐ ADR	☐ ADR

TOURING Planner

DAY: ___/___	DAY: ___/___	DAY: ___/___	DAY: ___/___
PARK:	PARK:	PARK:	PARK:
to EMH: am/pm	to EMH: am/pm	to EMH: am/pm	to EMH: am/pm
Crowd Level:	Crowd Level:	Crowd Level:	Crowd Level:

RIDES			
☐ FP+	☐ FP+	☐ FP+	☐ FP+
☐ FP+	☐ FP+	☐ FP+	☐ FP+
☐ FP+	☐ FP+	☐ FP+	☐ FP+
☐ FP+	☐ FP+	☐ FP+	☐ FP+
☐ FP+	☐ FP+	☐ FP+	☐ FP+

SHOWS/PARADES			
☐ FP+	☐ FP+	☐ FP+	☐ FP+
☐ FP+	☐ FP+	☐ FP+	☐ FP+
☐ FP+	☐ FP+	☐ FP+	☐ FP+

CHARACTER EXPERIENCE			
☐ FP+	☐ FP+	☐ FP+	☐ FP+
☐ FP+	☐ FP+	☐ FP+	☐ FP+

DINING			
☐ ADR	☐ ADR	☐ ADR	☐ ADR
☐ ADR	☐ ADR	☐ ADR	☐ ADR
☐ ADR	☐ ADR	☐ ADR	☐ ADR

TOURING Planner

DAY: ___/___	DAY: ___/___	DAY: ___/___	DAY: ___/___
PARK:	PARK:	PARK:	PARK:
to EMH: am/pm	to EMH: am/pm	to EMH: am/pm	to EMH: am/pm
Crowd Level:	Crowd Level:	Crowd Level:	Crowd Level:

RIDES

☐ FP+	☐ FP+	☐ FP+	☐ FP+
☐ FP+	☐ FP+	☐ FP+	☐ FP+
☐ FP+	☐ FP+	☐ FP+	☐ FP+
☐ FP+	☐ FP+	☐ FP+	☐ FP+
☐ FP+	☐ FP+	☐ FP+	☐ FP+

SHOWS/PARADES

☐ FP+	☐ FP+	☐ FP+	☐ FP+
☐ FP+	☐ FP+	☐ FP+	☐ FP+
☐ FP+	☐ FP+	☐ FP+	☐ FP+

CHARACTER EXPERIENCE

☐ FP+	☐ FP+	☐ FP+	☐ FP+
☐ FP+	☐ FP+	☐ FP+	☐ FP+

DINING

☐ ADR	☐ ADR	☐ ADR	☐ ADR
☐ ADR	☐ ADR	☐ ADR	☐ ADR
☐ ADR	☐ ADR	☐ ADR	☐ ADR

TOURING Planner

Day: ___ / ___	Day: ___ / ___	Day: ___ / ___	Day: ___ / ___
Park:	Park:	Park:	Park:
to EMH: am/pm	to EMH: am/pm	to EMH: am/pm	to EMH: am/pm
Crowd Level:	Crowd Level:	Crowd Level:	Crowd Level:

Rides

☐ FP+	☐ FP+	☐ FP+	☐ FP+
☐ FP+	☐ FP+	☐ FP+	☐ FP+
☐ FP+	☐ FP+	☐ FP+	☐ FP+
☐ FP+	☐ FP+	☐ FP+	☐ FP+
☐ FP+	☐ FP+	☐ FP+	☐ FP+

Shows/Parades

☐ FP+	☐ FP+	☐ FP+	☐ FP+
☐ FP+	☐ FP+	☐ FP+	☐ FP+
☐ FP+	☐ FP+	☐ FP+	☐ FP+

Character Experience

☐ FP+	☐ FP+	☐ FP+	☐ FP+
☐ FP+	☐ FP+	☐ FP+	☐ FP+

Dining

☐ ADR	☐ ADR	☐ ADR	☐ ADR
☐ ADR	☐ ADR	☐ ADR	☐ ADR
☐ ADR	☐ ADR	☐ ADR	☐ ADR

TOURING Planner

DAY: ___ / ___	DAY: ___ / ___	DAY: ___ / ___	DAY: ___ / ___
PARK:	PARK:	PARK:	PARK:
to EMH: am/pm	to EMH: am/pm	to EMH: am/pm	to EMH: am/pm
Crowd Level:	Crowd Level:	Crowd Level:	Crowd Level:

RIDES

☐ FP+	☐ FP+	☐ FP+	☐ FP+
☐ FP+	☐ FP+	☐ FP+	☐ FP+
☐ FP+	☐ FP+	☐ FP+	☐ FP+
☐ FP+	☐ FP+	☐ FP+	☐ FP+
☐ FP+	☐ FP+	☐ FP+	☐ FP+

SHOWS/PARADES

☐ FP+	☐ FP+	☐ FP+	☐ FP+
☐ FP+	☐ FP+	☐ FP+	☐ FP+
☐ FP+	☐ FP+	☐ FP+	☐ FP+

CHARACTER EXPERIENCE

☐ FP+	☐ FP+	☐ FP+	☐ FP+
☐ FP+	☐ FP+	☐ FP+	☐ FP+

DINING

☐ ADR	☐ ADR	☐ ADR	☐ ADR
☐ ADR	☐ ADR	☐ ADR	☐ ADR
☐ ADR	☐ ADR	☐ ADR	☐ ADR

DINING & FASTPASS Selections

ADR Date:	DINING PLAN:	FP+ SELECTION DATE:

DAY: ___/___	DAY: ___/___	DAY: ___/___	DAY: ___/___
FAST PASS ATTRACTION	FAST PASS ATTRACTION	FAST PASS ATTRACTION	FAST PASS ATTRACTION
: 📍	: 📍	: 📍	: 📍
FAST PASS ATTRACTION	FAST PASS ATTRACTION	FAST PASS ATTRACTION	FAST PASS ATTRACTION
: 📍	: 📍	: 📍	: 📍
FAST PASS ATTRACTION	FAST PASS ATTRACTION	FAST PASS ATTRACTION	FAST PASS ATTRACTION
: 📍	: 📍	: 📍	: 📍

·················· Dining ··················

BREAKFAST	BREAKFAST	BREAKFAST	BREAKFAST
: 📍	: 📍	: 📍	: 📍
Confirmation:	Confirmation:	Confirmation:	Confirmation:
Credits:	Credits:	Credits:	Credits:
LUNCH	LUNCH	LUNCH	LUNCH
: 📍	: 📍	: 📍	: 📍
Confirmation:	Confirmation:	Confirmation:	Confirmation:
Credits:	Credits:	Credits:	Credits:
DINNER	DINNER	DINNER	DINNER
: 📍	: 📍	: 📍	: 📍
Confirmation:	Confirmation:	Confirmation:	Confirmation:
Credits:	Credits:	Credits:	Credits:

NOTES

DINING & FASTPASS Selections

ADR Date: _____   Dining Plan: _____   FP+ Selection Date: _____

Day: ___/___	Day: ___/___	Day: ___/___	Day: ___/___
Fast Pass Attraction	**Fast Pass Attraction**	**Fast Pass Attraction**	**Fast Pass Attraction**
:	:	:	:
Fast Pass Attraction	**Fast Pass Attraction**	**Fast Pass Attraction**	**Fast Pass Attraction**
:	:	:	:
Fast Pass Attraction	**Fast Pass Attraction**	**Fast Pass Attraction**	**Fast Pass Attraction**
:	:	:	:

··· Dining ···

Breakfast	Breakfast	Breakfast	Breakfast
:	:	:	:
Confirmation:	Confirmation:	Confirmation:	Confirmation:
Credits:	Credits:	Credits:	Credits:
Lunch	Lunch	Lunch	Lunch
:	:	:	:
Confirmation:	Confirmation:	Confirmation:	Confirmation:
Credits:	Credits:	Credits:	Credits:
Dinner	Dinner	Dinner	Dinner
:	:	:	:
Confirmation:	Confirmation:	Confirmation:	Confirmation:
Credits:	Credits:	Credits:	Credits:

Notes

DINING & FASTPASS Selections

ADR Date: _____   Dining Plan: _____   FP+ Selection Date: _____

Day: ___ /___	Day: ___ /___	Day: ___ /___	Day: ___ /___
Fast Pass Attraction	Fast Pass Attraction	Fast Pass Attraction	Fast Pass Attraction
: ⦿	: ⦿	: ⦿	: ⦿
Fast Pass Attraction	Fast Pass Attraction	Fast Pass Attraction	Fast Pass Attraction
: ⦿	: ⦿	: ⦿	: ⦿
Fast Pass Attraction	Fast Pass Attraction	Fast Pass Attraction	Fast Pass Attraction
: ⦿	: ⦿	: ⦿	: ⦿

· Dining ·

Breakfast	Breakfast	Breakfast	Breakfast
: ⦿	: ⦿	: ⦿	: ⦿
Confirmation:	Confirmation:	Confirmation:	Confirmation:
Credits:	Credits:	Credits:	Credits:
Lunch	Lunch	Lunch	Lunch
: ⦿	: ⦿	: ⦿	: ⦿
Confirmation:	Confirmation:	Confirmation:	Confirmation:
Credits:	Credits:	Credits:	Credits:
Dinner	Dinner	Dinner	Dinner
: ⦿	: ⦿	: ⦿	: ⦿
Confirmation:	Confirmation:	Confirmation:	Confirmation:
Credits:	Credits:	Credits:	Credits:

Notes

DINING & FASTPASS Selections

ADR Date: _____ DINING PLAN: _____ FP+ SELECTION DATE: _____

DAY: ___/___	DAY: ___/___	DAY: ___/___	DAY: ___/___
FAST PASS ATTRACTION	FAST PASS ATTRACTION	FAST PASS ATTRACTION	FAST PASS ATTRACTION
:	:	:	:
FAST PASS ATTRACTION	FAST PASS ATTRACTION	FAST PASS ATTRACTION	FAST PASS ATTRACTION
:	:	:	:
FAST PASS ATTRACTION	FAST PASS ATTRACTION	FAST PASS ATTRACTION	FAST PASS ATTRACTION
:	:	:	:

············· Dining ·············

BREAKFAST	BREAKFAST	BREAKFAST	BREAKFAST
:	:	:	:
Confirmation:	Confirmation:	Confirmation:	Confirmation:
Credits:	Credits:	Credits:	Credits:
LUNCH	LUNCH	LUNCH	LUNCH
:	:	:	:
Confirmation:	Confirmation:	Confirmation:	Confirmation:
Credits:	Credits:	Credits:	Credits:
DINNER	DINNER	DINNER	DINNER
:	:	:	:
Confirmation:	Confirmation:	Confirmation:	Confirmation:
Credits:	Credits:	Credits:	Credits:

NOTES

DINING & FAST PASS Selections

DAY: ___ / ___	DAY: ___ / ___	DAY: ___ / ___	DAY: ___ / ___
FAST PASS ATTRACTION	FAST PASS ATTRACTION	FAST PASS ATTRACTION	FAST PASS ATTRACTION
:	:	:	:
FAST PASS ATTRACTION	FAST PASS ATTRACTION	FAST PASS ATTRACTION	FAST PASS ATTRACTION
:	:	:	:
FAST PASS ATTRACTION	FAST PASS ATTRACTION	FAST PASS ATTRACTION	FAST PASS ATTRACTION
:	:	:	:

· *Dining* ·

BREAKFAST	BREAKFAST	BREAKFAST	BREAKFAST
:	:	:	:
Confirmation:	Confirmation:	Confirmation:	Confirmation:
Credits:	Credits:	Credits:	Credits:
LUNCH	LUNCH	LUNCH	LUNCH
:	:	:	:
Confirmation:	Confirmation:	Confirmation:	Confirmation:
Credits:	Credits:	Credits:	Credits:
DINNER	DINNER	DINNER	DINNER
:	:	:	:
Confirmation:	Confirmation:	Confirmation:	Confirmation:
Credits:	Credits:	Credits:	Credits:

Notes

TOURING Plan

DAY: ___/___	DAY: ___/___	DAY: ___/___	DAY: ___/___

··· Breakfast ···

MORNING PARK/ACTIVITY

··· Lunch ···

AFTERNOON PARK/ACTIVITY

··· Dinner ···

EVENING PARK/ACTIVITY

TOURING Plan

Day: ___/___	Day: ___/___	Day: ___/___	Day: ___/___

······················· Breakfast ·······················

Morning Park/Activity

······················· Lunch ·······················

Afternoon Park/Activity

······················· Dinner ·······················

Evening Park/Activity

TOURING Plan

·· Breakfast ··

MORNING PARK/ACTIVITY

·· Lunch ··

AFTERNOON PARK/ACTIVITY

·· Dinner ··

EVENING PARK/ACTIVITY

TOURING Plan

.... Breakfast ....

MORNING PARK/ACTIVITY

.... Lunch ....

AFTERNOON PARK/ACTIVITY

.... Dinner ....

EVENING PARK/ACTIVITY

TOURING Plan

DAY: ___ /___	DAY: ___ /___	DAY: ___ /___	DAY: ___ /___

························· Breakfast ·························

MORNING PARK/ACTIVITY

·························· Lunch ··························

AFTERNOON PARK/ACTIVITY

·························· Dinner ··························

EVENING PARK/ACTIVITY

TODAY'S Plan

PARK
_____

POSTED HOURS
____ : ____ TO ____ : ____

EXTRA MAGIC HOURS
☐ AM   ☐ PM

SCHEDULE

7:00

8:00

9:00

10:00

11:00

12:00

1:00

2:00

3:00

4:00

5:00

6:00

7:00

8:00

9:00

10:00

11:00

DINING   RESERVATION

Breakfast:

Lunch:

Dinner:

Snacks:

RIDES   FAST PASS

CHARACTERS TO MEET

☐

☐

☐

☐

☐

☐

NOTES

HIGHLIGHTS   RATING

TODAY'S Plan

DATE_____

PARK
_____

POSTED HOURS
____ : ____ TO ____ : ____

EXTRA MAGIC HOURS
☐ AM   ☐ PM

SCHEDULE	
7:00	
8:00	
9:00	
10:00	
11:00	
12:00	
1:00	
2:00	
3:00	
4:00	
5:00	
6:00	
7:00	
8:00	
9:00	
10:00	
11:00	

DINING	RESERVATION
Breakfast:	
Lunch:	
Dinner:	
Snacks:	

RIDES	FAST PASS

CHARACTERS TO MEET

- ☐
- ☐
- ☐
- ☐
- ☐
- ☐

NOTES

HIGHLIGHTS

RATING
_____

TODAY'S Plan

DATE_____

POSTED HOURS

____ : ____ TO ____ : ____

EXTRA MAGIC HOURS

☐ AM   ☐ PM

SCHEDULE

7:00

8:00

9:00

10:00

11:00

12:00

1:00

2:00

3:00

4:00

5:00

6:00

7:00

8:00

9:00

10:00

11:00

DINING   RESERVATION

Breakfast:

Lunch:

Dinner:

Snacks:

RIDES   FAST PASS

CHARACTERS TO MEET

☐
☐
☐
☐
☐
☐

NOTES

HIGHLIGHTS   RATING

TODAY'S Plan

PARK	POSTED HOURS	EXTRA MAGIC HOURS
_____	____ : ____ TO ____ : ____	☐ AM ☐ PM

SCHEDULE

7:00

8:00

9:00

10:00

11:00

12:00

1:00

2:00

3:00

4:00

5:00

6:00

7:00

8:00

9:00

10:00

11:00

DINING   RESERVATION

Breakfast:

Lunch:

Dinner:

Snacks:

RIDES   FAST PASS

CHARACTERS TO MEET

☐

☐

☐

☐

☐

☐

NOTES

HIGHLIGHTS   RATING

TODAY'S Plan

DATE_____

PARK
_____

POSTED HOURS
___ : ___ TO ___ : ___

EXTRA MAGIC HOURS
☐ AM   ☐ PM

SCHEDULE

7:00

8:00

9:00

10:00

11:00

12:00

1:00

2:00

3:00

4:00

5:00

6:00

7:00

8:00

9:00

10:00

11:00

DINING   RESERVATION

Breakfast:

Lunch:

Dinner:

Snacks:

RIDES   FAST PASS

CHARACTERS TO MEET

☐

☐

☐

☐

☐

☐

NOTES

HIGHLIGHTS   *RATING*

TODAY'S Plan

DATE_____

POSTED HOURS

____ : ____ TO ____ : ____

EXTRA MAGIC HOURS

☐ AM   ☐ PM

SCHEDULE

7:00

8:00

9:00

10:00

11:00

12:00

1:00

2:00

3:00

4:00

5:00

6:00

7:00

8:00

9:00

10:00

11:00

DINING   RESERVATION

Breakfast:

Lunch:

Dinner:

Snacks:

RIDES   FAST PASS

CHARACTERS TO MEET

☐

☐

☐

☐

☐

☐

NOTES

HIGHLIGHTS   RATING

_ _ _ _ _

TODAY'S Plan

DATE_____

PARK
_____

POSTED HOURS
____ : ____ TO ____ : ____

EXTRA MAGIC HOURS
☐ AM   ☐ PM

SCHEDULE

7:00

8:00

9:00

10:00

11:00

12:00

1:00

2:00

3:00

4:00

5:00

6:00

7:00

8:00

9:00

10:00

11:00

DINING   RESERVATION

Breakfast:

Lunch:

Dinner:

Snacks:

RIDES   FAST PASS

CHARACTERS TO MEET

☐

☐

☐

☐

☐

☐

NOTES

HIGHLIGHTS   RATING

TODAY'S Plan

DATE_____

PARK
_____

POSTED HOURS
____ : ____ TO ____ : ____

EXTRA MAGIC HOURS
☐ AM   ☐ PM

SCHEDULE

7:00

8:00

9:00

10:00

11:00

12:00

1:00

2:00

3:00

4:00

5:00

6:00

7:00

8:00

9:00

10:00

11:00

DINING   RESERVATION

Breakfast:

Lunch:

Dinner:

Snacks:

RIDES   FAST PASS

CHARACTERS TO MEET

☐
☐
☐
☐
☐
☐

NOTES

HIGHLIGHTS   *RATING*

TODAY'S Plan

DATE_____

PARK

_____

POSTED HOURS

____ : ____ TO ____ : ____

EXTRA MAGIC HOURS

☐ AM   ☐ PM

SCHEDULE

7:00

8:00

9:00

10:00

11:00

12:00

1:00

2:00

3:00

4:00

5:00

6:00

7:00

8:00

9:00

10:00

11:00

DINING   RESERVATION

Breakfast:

Lunch:

Dinner:

Snacks:

RIDES   FAST PASS

CHARACTERS TO MEET

☐

☐

☐

☐

☐

☐

NOTES

HIGHLIGHTS   *RATING*

TODAY's Plan

DATE_____

POSTED HOURS

____ : ____ TO ____ : ____

EXTRA MAGIC HOURS

☐ AM   ☐ PM

SCHEDULE

7:00

8:00

9:00

10:00

11:00

12:00

1:00

2:00

3:00

4:00

5:00

6:00

7:00

8:00

9:00

10:00

11:00

DINING   RESERVATION

Breakfast:

Lunch:

Dinner:

Snacks:

RIDES   FAST PASS

CHARACTERS TO MEET

☐

☐

☐

☐

☐

☐

NOTES

HIGHLIGHTS   RATING

TODAY'S Memories

TODAY WAS: ☐ REALLY FUN ☐ AWESOME ☐ THE BEST DAY EVER!

WE WENT TO:

MY FAVORITE RIDES AND ATTRACTION WERE:

CHARACTERS I SAW:

The **BEST** part of my day was...

SOUVENIRS I BOUGHT OR WANT TO BUY:

BEST FOOD OF THE DAY:

I CAN'T WAIT FOR TOMORROW:

TODAY'S Memories

TODAY WAS: ☐ REALLY FUN   ☐ AWESOME   ☐ THE BEST DAY EVER!

WE WENT TO:

MY FAVORITE RIDES AND ATTRACTION WERE:

CHARACTERS I SAW:

The **BEST** part of
my day was...

SOUVENIRS I BOUGHT OR WANT TO BUY:

BEST FOOD OF THE DAY:

I CAN'T WAIT FOR TOMORROW:

TODAY'S Memories

DATE_____

TODAY WAS: [ ] REALLY FUN [ ] AWESOME [ ] THE BEST DAY EVER!

WE WENT TO:

_____

_____

MY FAVORITE RIDES AND ATTRACTION WERE:

_____

_____

_____

_____

_____

_____

CHARACTERS I SAW:

_____

_____

_____

_____

The **BEST** part of
my day was...

SOUVENIRS I BOUGHT OR WANT TO BUY:

_____

_____

BEST FOOD OF THE DAY:

I CAN'T WAIT FOR TOMORROW:

_____

_____

_____

_____

TODAY'S Memories

DATE_____

TODAY WAS: ☐ REALLY FUN   ☐ AWESOME   ☐ THE BEST DAY EVER!

WE WENT TO:

MY FAVORITE RIDES AND ATTRACTION WERE:

CHARACTERS I SAW:

The **BEST** part of my day was...

SOUVENIRS I BOUGHT OR WANT TO BUY:

BEST FOOD OF THE DAY:

I CAN'T WAIT FOR TOMORROW:

TODAY'S Memories

DATE_____

TODAY WAS: ☐ REALLY FUN   ☐ AWESOME   ☐ THE BEST DAY EVER!

WE WENT TO:

MY FAVORITE RIDES AND ATTRACTION WERE:

CHARACTERS I SAW:

The BEST part of my day was...

SOUVENIRS I BOUGHT OR WANT TO BUY:

BEST FOOD OF THE DAY:

I CAN'T WAIT FOR TOMORROW:

TODAY'S Memories

TODAY WAS: ☐ REALLY FUN ☐ AWESOME ☐ THE BEST DAY EVER!

WE WENT TO:

MY FAVORITE RIDES AND ATTRACTION WERE:

CHARACTERS I SAW:

The **BEST** part of
my day was...

SOUVENIRS I BOUGHT OR WANT TO BUY:

BEST FOOD OF THE DAY:

I CAN'T WAIT FOR TOMORROW:

TODAY'S Memories

DATE_____

WE WENT TO:

MY FAVORITE RIDES AND ATTRACTION WERE:

The **BEST** part of
my day was...

CHARACTERS I SAW:

SOUVENIRS I BOUGHT OR WANT TO BUY:

BEST FOOD OF THE DAY:

I CAN'T WAIT FOR TOMORROW:

TODAY'S Memories

TODAY WAS: ☐ REALLY FUN ☐ AWESOME ☐ THE BEST DAY EVER!

WE WENT TO:

MY FAVORITE RIDES AND ATTRACTION WERE:

CHARACTERS I SAW:

The **BEST** part of
my day was...

SOUVENIRS I BOUGHT OR WANT TO BUY:

BEST FOOD OF THE DAY:

I CAN'T WAIT FOR TOMORROW:

TODAY'S Memories

DATE_____

TODAY WAS: ☐ REALLY FUN ☐ AWESOME ☐ THE BEST DAY EVER!

WE WENT TO:

MY FAVORITE RIDES AND ATTRACTION WERE:

CHARACTERS I SAW:

The **BEST** part of
my day was...

SOUVENIRS I BOUGHT OR WANT TO BUY:

BEST FOOD OF THE DAY:

I CAN'T WAIT FOR TOMORROW:

TODAY'S Memories

DATE_____

TODAY WAS: ☐ REALLY FUN ☐ AWESOME ☐ THE BEST DAY EVER!

WE WENT TO:

MY FAVORITE RIDES AND ATTRACTION WERE:

CHARACTERS I SAW:

The **BEST** part of
my day was...

SOUVENIRS I BOUGHT OR WANT TO BUY:

BEST FOOD OF THE DAY:

I CAN'T WAIT FOR TOMORROW:

OUTFIT Planner

Day 1
°
Packed ☐

Clothes:

Destination:
Shoes:

Activity:
Accessories:

Day 2
°
Packed ☐

Clothes:

Destination:
Shoes:

Activity:
Accessories:

Day 3
°
Packed ☐

Clothes:

Destination:
Shoes:

Activity:
Accessories:

Day 4
°
Packed ☐

Clothes:

Destination:
Shoes:

Activity:
Accessories:

Day 5
°
Packed ☐

Clothes:

Destination:
Shoes:

Activity:
Accessories:

Day 6
°
Packed ☐

Clothes:

Destination:
Shoes:

Activity:
Accessories:

Day 7
°
Packed ☐

Clothes:

Destination:
Shoes:

Activity:
Accessories:

EXTRAS:

NEED TO BUY:

OUTFIT Planner

Day 1 🌡 ° ☀ ⛅ 🌧 ❄   *Packed* ☐

Clothes: _____

Destination: _____   Shoes: _____

Activity: _____   Accessories: _____

Day 2 🌡 ° ☀ ⛅ 🌧 ❄   *Packed* ☐

Clothes: _____

Destination: _____   Shoes: _____

Activity: _____   Accessories: _____

Day 3 🌡 ° ☀ ⛅ 🌧 ❄   *Packed* ☐

Clothes: _____

Destination: _____   Shoes: _____

Activity: _____   Accessories: _____

Day 4 🌡 ° ☀ ⛅ 🌧 ❄   *Packed* ☐

Clothes: _____

Destination: _____   Shoes: _____

Activity: _____   Accessories: _____

Day 5 🌡 ° ☀ ⛅ 🌧 ❄   *Packed* ☐

Clothes: _____

Destination: _____   Shoes: _____

Activity: _____   Accessories: _____

Day 6 🌡 ° ☀ ⛅ 🌧 ❄   *Packed* ☐

Clothes: _____

Destination: _____   Shoes: _____

Activity: _____   Accessories: _____

Day 7 🌡 ° ☀ ⛅ 🌧 ❄   *Packed* ☐

Clothes: _____

Destination: _____   Shoes: _____

Activity: _____   Accessories: _____

EXTRAS:

NEED TO BUY:

OUTFIT Planner

Day 1

🌡 ° ☀ ⛅ 🌧 ❄   *Packed* ☐

Clothes: _____

Destination: _____   Shoes: _____

Activity: _____   Accessories: _____

Day 2

🌡 ° ☀ ⛅ 🌧 ❄   *Packed* ☐

Clothes: _____

Destination: _____   Shoes: _____

Activity: _____   Accessories: _____

Day 3

🌡 ° ☀ ⛅ 🌧 ❄   *Packed* ☐

Clothes: _____

Destination: _____   Shoes: _____

Activity: _____   Accessories: _____

Day 4

🌡 ° ☀ ⛅ 🌧 ❄   *Packed* ☐

Clothes: _____

Destination: _____   Shoes: _____

Activity: _____   Accessories: _____

Day 5

🌡 ° ☀ ⛅ 🌧 ❄   *Packed* ☐

Clothes: _____

Destination: _____   Shoes: _____

Activity: _____   Accessories: _____

Day 6

🌡 ° ☀ ⛅ 🌧 ❄   *Packed* ☐

Clothes: _____

Destination: _____   Shoes: _____

Activity: _____   Accessories: _____

Day 7

🌡 ° ☀ ⛅ 🌧 ❄   *Packed* ☐

Clothes: _____

Destination: _____   Shoes: _____

Activity: _____   Accessories: _____

EXTRAS:

NEED TO BUY:

OUTFIT Planner

Day 1
° ☀ ⛅ 🌧 ❄
Packed ☐
Clothes:
Destination:
Shoes:
Activity:
Accessories:

Day 2
° ☀ ⛅ 🌧 ❄
Packed ☐
Clothes:
Destination:
Shoes:
Activity:
Accessories:

Day 3
° ☀ ⛅ 🌧 ❄
Packed ☐
Clothes:
Destination:
Shoes:
Activity:
Accessories:

Day 4
° ☀ ⛅ 🌧 ❄
Packed ☐
Clothes:
Destination:
Shoes:
Activity:
Accessories:

Day 5
° ☀ ⛅ 🌧 ❄
Packed ☐
Clothes:
Destination:
Shoes:
Activity:
Accessories:

Day 6
° ☀ ⛅ 🌧 ❄
Packed ☐
Clothes:
Destination:
Shoes:
Activity:
Accessories:

Day 7
° ☀ ⛅ 🌧 ❄
Packed ☐
Clothes:
Destination:
Shoes:
Activity:
Accessories:

EXTRAS:

NEED TO BUY:

OUTFIT Planner

Day 1
° Packed ☐

Clothes:

Destination: | Shoes:

Activity: | Accessories:

Day 2
° Packed ☐

Clothes:

Destination: | Shoes:

Activity: | Accessories:

Day 3
° Packed ☐

Clothes:

Destination: | Shoes:

Activity: | Accessories:

Day 4
° Packed ☐

Clothes:

Destination: | Shoes:

Activity: | Accessories:

Day 5
° Packed ☐

Clothes:

Destination: | Shoes:

Activity: | Accessories:

Day 6
° Packed ☐

Clothes:

Destination: | Shoes:

Activity: | Accessories:

Day 7
° Packed ☐

Clothes:

Destination: | Shoes:

Activity: | Accessories:

EXTRAS:

NEED TO BUY:

OUTFIT Planner

Day 1   °   ☀ ⛅ 🌧 ❄   *Packed* ☐

Clothes:

Destination: Shoes:

Activity: Accessories:

Day 2   °   ☀ ⛅ 🌧 ❄   *Packed* ☐

Clothes:

Destination: Shoes:

Activity: Accessories:

Day 3   °   ☀ ⛅ 🌧 ❄   *Packed* ☐

Clothes:

Destination: Shoes:

Activity: Accessories:

Day 4   °   ☀ ⛅ 🌧 ❄   *Packed* ☐

Clothes:

Destination: Shoes:

Activity: Accessories:

Day 5   °   ☀ ⛅ 🌧 ❄   *Packed* ☐

Clothes:

Destination: Shoes:

Activity: Accessories:

Day 6   °   ☀ ⛅ 🌧 ❄   *Packed* ☐

Clothes:

Destination: Shoes:

Activity: Accessories:

Day 7   °   ☀ ⛅ 🌧 ❄   *Packed* ☐

Clothes:

Destination: Shoes:

Activity: Accessories:

EXTRAS:

NEED TO BUY:

OUTFIT Planner

Day 1
° ☀ ⛅ 🌧 ❄
Packed ☐

Clothes: _____

Destination: _____
Shoes: _____

Activity: _____
Accessories: _____

Day 2
° ☀ ⛅ 🌧 ❄
Packed ☐

Clothes: _____

Destination: _____
Shoes: _____

Activity: _____
Accessories: _____

Day 3
° ☀ ⛅ 🌧 ❄
Packed ☐

Clothes: _____

Destination: _____
Shoes: _____

Activity: _____
Accessories: _____

Day 4
° ☀ ⛅ 🌧 ❄
Packed ☐

Clothes: _____

Destination: _____
Shoes: _____

Activity: _____
Accessories: _____

Day 5
° ☀ ⛅ 🌧 ❄
Packed ☐

Clothes: _____

Destination: _____
Shoes: _____

Activity: _____
Accessories: _____

Day 6
° ☀ ⛅ 🌧 ❄
Packed ☐

Clothes: _____

Destination: _____
Shoes: _____

Activity: _____
Accessories: _____

Day 7
° ☀ ⛅ 🌧 ❄
Packed ☐

Clothes: _____

Destination: _____
Shoes: _____

Activity: _____
Accessories: _____

EXTRAS:

NEED TO BUY:

OUTFIT Planner

Day 1 🌡 ° ☀ ⛅ 🌧 ❄   *Packed* ☐

Clothes:

Destination: Shoes:

Activity: Accessories:

EXTRAS:

Day 2 🌡 ° ☀ ⛅ 🌧 ❄   *Packed* ☐

Clothes:

Destination: Shoes:

Activity: Accessories:

Day 3 🌡 ° ☀ ⛅ 🌧 ❄   *Packed* ☐

Clothes:

Destination: Shoes:

Activity: Accessories:

Day 4 🌡 ° ☀ ⛅ 🌧 ❄   *Packed* ☐

Clothes:

Destination: Shoes:

NEED TO BUY:

Activity: Accessories:

Day 5 🌡 ° ☀ ⛅ 🌧 ❄   *Packed* ☐

Clothes:

Destination: Shoes:

Activity: Accessories:

Day 6 🌡 ° ☀ ⛅ 🌧 ❄   *Packed* ☐

Clothes:

Destination: Shoes:

Activity: Accessories:

Day 7 🌡 ° ☀ ⛅ 🌧 ❄   *Packed* ☐

Clothes:

Destination: Shoes:

Activity: Accessories:

OUTFIT Planner

Day 1

° ☀ ⛅ 🌧 ❄   *Packed* ☐

Clothes: _____

Destination: _____

Shoes: _____

Activity: _____

Accessories: _____

Day 2

° ☀ ⛅ 🌧 ❄   *Packed* ☐

Clothes: _____

Destination: _____

Shoes: _____

Activity: _____

Accessories: _____

Day 3

° ☀ ⛅ 🌧 ❄   *Packed* ☐

Clothes: _____

Destination: _____

Shoes: _____

Activity: _____

Accessories: _____

Day 4

° ☀ ⛅ 🌧 ❄   *Packed* ☐

Clothes: _____

Destination: _____

Shoes: _____

Activity: _____

Accessories: _____

Day 5

° ☀ ⛅ 🌧 ❄   *Packed* ☐

Clothes: _____

Destination: _____

Shoes: _____

Activity: _____

Accessories: _____

Day 6

° ☀ ⛅ 🌧 ❄   *Packed* ☐

Clothes: _____

Destination: _____

Shoes: _____

Activity: _____

Accessories: _____

Day 7

° ☀ ⛅ 🌧 ❄   *Packed* ☐

Clothes: _____

Destination: _____

Shoes: _____

Activity: _____

Accessories: _____

EXTRAS:

NEED TO BUY:

OUTFIT Planner

Day 1

Destination:

Activity:

Clothes:

Shoes:

Accessories:

Packed ☐

Day 2

Destination:

Activity:

Clothes:

Shoes:

Accessories:

Packed ☐

Day 3

Destination:

Activity:

Clothes:

Shoes:

Accessories:

Packed ☐

Day 4

Destination:

Activity:

Clothes:

Shoes:

Accessories:

Packed ☐

Day 5

Destination:

Activity:

Clothes:

Shoes:

Accessories:

Packed ☐

Day 6

Destination:

Activity:

Clothes:

Shoes:

Accessories:

Packed ☐

Day 7

Destination:

Activity:

Clothes:

Shoes:

Accessories:

Packed ☐

EXTRAS:

NEED TO BUY:

FAMILY OUTFIT Planner

TRIP DATES: ____/____/____ TO ____/____/____   NUMBER OF OUTFITS: _____

	ACTIVITIES	TRAVELER	TOPS	BOTTOMS	SHOES
DAY 1					
			PACKED! ☐	PACKED! ☐	PACKED! ☐
DAY 2					
			PACKED! ☐	PACKED! ☐	PACKED! ☐
DAY 3					
			PACKED! ☐	PACKED! ☐	PACKED! ☐
DAY 4					
			PACKED! ☐	PACKED! ☐	PACKED! ☐

FAMILY OUTFIT Planner

	ACTIVITIES	TRAVELER	TOPS	BOTTOMS	SHOES
DAY 1					
			PACKED!	PACKED!	PACKED!
DAY 2					
			PACKED!	PACKED!	PACKED!
DAY 3					
			PACKED!	PACKED!	PACKED!
DAY 4					
			PACKED!	PACKED!	PACKED!

FAMILY OUTFIT Planner

TRIP DATES: ____/____/____ TO ____/____/____   NUMBER OF OUTFITS: _____

	ACTIVITIES	TRAVELER	TOPS	BOTTOMS	SHOES
DAY 1					
			PACKED! ☐	PACKED! ☐	PACKED! ☐
DAY 2					
			PACKED! ☐	PACKED! ☐	PACKED! ☐
DAY 3					
			PACKED! ☐	PACKED! ☐	PACKED! ☐
DAY 4					
			PACKED! ☐	PACKED! ☐	PACKED! ☐

FAMILY OUTFIT Planner

TRIP DATES: ___/___/___ TO ___/___/___   NUMBER OF OUTFITS: _____

	ACTIVITIES	TRAVELER	TOPS	BOTTOMS	SHOES
DAY 1					
			PACKED! ☐	PACKED! ☐	PACKED! ☐
DAY 2					
			PACKED! ☐	PACKED! ☐	PACKED! ☐
DAY 3					
			PACKED! ☐	PACKED! ☐	PACKED! ☐
DAY 4					
			PACKED! ☐	PACKED! ☐	PACKED! ☐

FAMILY OUTFIT Planner

TRIP DATES: ___/___/___ TO ___/___/___   NUMBER OF OUTFITS: _____

	ACTIVITIES	TRAVELER	TOPS	BOTTOMS	SHOES
DAY 1					
			PACKED! ▨	PACKED! ▨	PACKED! ▨
DAY 2					
			PACKED! ▨	PACKED! ▨	PACKED! ▨
DAY 3					
			PACKED! ▨	PACKED! ▨	PACKED! ▨
DAY 4					
			PACKED! ▨	PACKED! ▨	PACKED! ▨

FAMILY OUTFIT Planner

TRIP DATES: ___/___/___ TO ___/___/___   NUMBER OF OUTFITS: _____

	ACTIVITIES	TRAVELER	TOPS	BOTTOMS	SHOES
DAY 1					
			PACKED! ☐	PACKED! ☐	PACKED! ☐
DAY 2					
			PACKED! ☐	PACKED! ☐	PACKED! ☐
DAY 3					
			PACKED! ☐	PACKED! ☐	PACKED! ☐
DAY 4					
			PACKED! ☐	PACKED! ☐	PACKED! ☐

FAMILY OUTFIT Planner

	ACTIVITIES	TRAVELER	TOPS	BOTTOMS	SHOES
DAY 1					
			PACKED! ☐	PACKED! ☐	PACKED! ☐
DAY 2					
			PACKED! ☐	PACKED! ☐	PACKED! ☐
DAY 3					
			PACKED! ☐	PACKED! ☐	PACKED! ☐
DAY 4					
			PACKED! ☐	PACKED! ☐	PACKED! ☐

FAMILY OUTFIT Planner

TRIP DATES: ___/___/___ TO ___/___/___   NUMBER OF OUTFITS: _____

ACTIVITIES	TRAVELER	TOPS	BOTTOMS	SHOES
DAY 1				
		PACKED!	PACKED!	PACKED!
DAY 2				
		PACKED!	PACKED!	PACKED!
DAY 3				
		PACKED!	PACKED!	PACKED!
DAY 4				
		PACKED!	PACKED!	PACKED!

FAMILY OUTFIT Planner

TRIP DATES: ____/____/____ TO ____/____/____   NUMBER OF OUTFITS: _____

	ACTIVITIES	TRAVELER	TOPS	BOTTOMS	SHOES
DAY 1					
			PACKED! ☐	PACKED! ☐	PACKED! ☐
DAY 2					
			PACKED! ☐	PACKED! ☐	PACKED! ☐
DAY 3					
			PACKED! ☐	PACKED! ☐	PACKED! ☐
DAY 4					
			PACKED! ☐	PACKED! ☐	PACKED! ☐

FAMILY OUTFIT Planner

TRIP DATES: ___/___/___ TO ___/___/___   NUMBER OF OUTFITS: _____

	ACTIVITIES	TRAVELER	TOPS	BOTTOMS	SHOES
DAY 5					
			PACKED! ☐	PACKED! ☐	PACKED! ☐
DAY 6					
			PACKED! ☐	PACKED! ☐	PACKED! ☐
DAY 7					
			PACKED! ☐	PACKED! ☐	PACKED! ☐
DAY 8					
			PACKED! ☐	PACKED! ☐	PACKED! ☐

PACKING Checklist

CLOTHING

✓	QTY	TOPS	✓	QTY	BASICS	✓	OUTERWEAR/SWIMWEAR	✓	OTHER
☐		Dressy	☐		Underwear	☐	Swimsuits/Cover-up	☐	
☐		Casual	☐		Socks	☐	Jacket/Sweatshirt	☐	
☐		T-shirts	☐		Bras/Undershirts	☐	Hat	☐	
☐		Exercise	☐		Sleepwear	☐		☐	

	QTY	BOTTOMS		QTY	ACCESSORIES		FOOTWEAR		
☐		Dress Pants	☐		Belts	☐	Dress Shoes	☐	
☐		Jeans	☐		Ties/Scarves	☐	Athletic/Walking Shoes	☐	
☐		Shorts	☐		Jewelry	☐	Sandals/Flip-flops	☐	
☐		Exercise	☐		Sunglasses	☐	Water Shoes	☐	

TOILETRIES

	HYGIENE		HAIR CARE		COSMETICS		MISC.
☐	Toothbrush/Paste	☐	Shampoo/Conditioner	☐	Face Wash	☐	Tweezers
☐	Dental Floss/Mouthwash	☐	Comb/Brush	☐	Moisturizer	☐	Nail Clippers/File
☐	Contacts/Saline	☐	Styling Products	☐	Makeup	☐	
☐	Deodorant	☐	Hairdryer	☐	Makeup Remover	☐	
☐	Soap/Body Wash	☐	Curling/Flat Iron/Dryer	☐	Perfume	☐	
☐	Feminine Products	☐	Hair Accessories	☐	Cotton Balls/Q-tips	☐	
☐		☐		☐		☐	

MISCELLANEOUS

	HEALTH		GEAR		ELECTRONICS		MISC.
☐	Medication/Vitamins	☐	Laundry Bag	☐	Laptop/Tablet	☐	Ear Plugs
☐	Pain Relievers	☐	Pop Up Hamper	☐	iPod/e-Reader	☐	Clothespins/Safety Pins
☐	Anti-nausea Pills	☐	Backpack/Beach Tote	☐	Chargers/Batteries	☐	Flashlight
☐	First Aid Kit	☐	Collapsible Cooler	☐	Camera	☐	Small Scissors
☐	Sunscreen	☐	Collapsible Storage Bins	☐		☐	

CARRY-ON

	TRAVEL ID/FUNDS/DOCS		TRAVEL DOCUMENTS		TRAVEL AIDS		MISC.
☐	Passport/Visa/ID	☐	Itinerary	☐	Ear Buds/Headphones	☐	Eye Drops
☐	Credit/ATM Cards	☐	Reservation Docs/Tickets	☐	Travel Blanket/Pillow	☐	
☐	Cash/Singles for Tips/Tolls	☐	Maps/Directions	☐	Food/Snacks	☐	
☐	Insurance Cards	☐		☐	In-Flight Medication	☐	
☐	Membership Cards (AAA, DVC)	☐		☐	Hand Sanitizer	☐	

PACKING Checklist

TRAVELER	DESTINATION	DAYS	WEATHER

🌡 _° ☀ ☁ 🌧

CLOTHING

✓	QTY	TOPS	✓	QTY	BASICS	✓	OUTERWEAR/SWIMWEAR	✓	OTHER
		Dressy			Underwear		Swimsuits/Cover-up		
		Casual			Socks		Jacket/Sweatshirt		
		T-shirts			Bras/Undershirts		Hat		
		Exercise			Sleepwear				

QTY	BOTTOMS	QTY	ACCESSORIES		FOOTWEAR
	Dress Pants		Belts		Dress Shoes
	Jeans		Ties/Scarves		Athletic/Walking Shoes
	Shorts		Jewelry		Sandals/Flip-flops
	Exercise		Sunglasses		Water Shoes

TOILETRIES

HYGIENE	HAIR CARE	COSMETICS	MISC.
☐ Toothbrush/Paste	☐ Shampoo/Conditioner	☐ Face Wash	☐ Tweezers
☐ Dental Floss/Mouthwash	☐ Comb/Brush	☐ Moisturizer	☐ Nail Clippers/File
☐ Contacts/Saline	☐ Styling Products	☐ Makeup	☐
☐ Deodorant	☐ Hairdryer	☐ Makeup Remover	☐
☐ Soap/Body Wash	☐ Curling/Flat Iron/Dryer	☐ Perfume	☐
☐ Feminine Products	☐ Hair Accessories	☐ Cotton Balls/Q-tips	☐
☐	☐	☐	☐

MISCELLANEOUS

HEALTH	GEAR	ELECTRONICS	MISC.
☐ Medication/Vitamins	☐ Laundry Bag	☐ Laptop/Tablet	☐ Ear Plugs
☐ Pain Relievers	☐ Pop Up Hamper	☐ iPod/e-Reader	☐ Clothespins/Safety Pins
☐ Anti-nausea Pills	☐ Backpack/Beach Tote	☐ Chargers/Batteries	☐ Flashlight
☐ First Aid Kit	☐ Collapsible Cooler	☐ Camera	☐ Small Scissors
☐ Sunscreen	☐ Collapsible Storage Bins	☐	☐

CARRY-ON

TRAVEL ID/FUNDS/DOCS	TRAVEL DOCUMENTS	TRAVEL AIDS	MISC.
Passport/Visa/ID	Itinerary	Ear Buds/Headphones	Eye Drops
Credit/ATM Cards	Reservation Docs/Tickets	Travel Blanket/Pillow	
Cash/Singles for Tips/Tolls	Maps/Directions	Food/Snacks	
Insurance Cards		In-Flight Medication	
Membership Cards (AAA, DVC)		Hand Sanitizer	

PACKING Checklist

TRAVELER	DESTINATION	DAYS	WEATHER

✓	QTY	TOPS	✓	QTY	BASICS	✓	OUTERWEAR/SWIMWEAR	✓	OTHER
☐		Dressy	☐		Underwear	☐	Swimsuits/Cover-up	☐	
☐		Casual	☐		Socks	☐	Jacket/Sweatshirt		
☐		T-shirts	☐		Bras/Undershirts	☐	Hat		
☐		Exercise	☐		Sleepwear				
			☐						

	QTY	BOTTOMS		QTY	ACCESSORIES		FOOTWEAR		
		Dress Pants	☐		Belts		Dress Shoes		
		Jeans	☐		Ties/Scarves		Athletic/Walking Shoes		
		Shorts	☐		Jewelry		Sandals/Flip-flops		
		Exercise			Sunglasses		Water Shoes		

CLOTHING

HYGIENE	HAIR CARE	COSMETICS	MISC.
☐ Toothbrush/Paste	☐ Shampoo/Conditioner	☐ Face Wash	☐ Tweezers
☐ Dental Floss/Mouthwash	☐ Comb/Brush	☐ Moisturizer	☐ Nail Clippers/File
☐ Contacts/Saline	☐ Styling Products	☐ Makeup	☐
☐ Deodorant	☐ Hairdryer	☐ Makeup Remover	☐
☐ Soap/Body Wash	☐ Curling/Flat Iron/Dryer	☐ Perfume	☐
☐ Feminine Products	☐ Hair Accessories	☐ Cotton Balls/Q-tips	☐
☐	☐	☐	☐

TOILETRIES

HEALTH	GEAR	ELECTRONICS	MISC.
☐ Medication/Vitamins	☐ Laundry Bag	☐ Laptop/Tablet	☐ Ear Plugs
☐ Pain Relievers	☐ Pop Up Hamper	☐ iPod/e-Reader	☐ Clothespins/Safety Pins
☐ Anti-nausea Pills	☐ Backpack/Beach Tote	☐ Chargers/Batteries	☐ Flashlight
☐ First Aid Kit	☐ Collapsible Cooler	☐ Camera	☐ Small Scissors
☐ Sunscreen	☐ Collapsible Storage Bins	☐	☐

MISCELLANEOUS

TRAVEL ID/FUNDS/DOCS	TRAVEL DOCUMENTS	TRAVEL AIDS	MISC.
☐ Passport/Visa/ID	☐ Itinerary	☐ Ear Buds/Headphones	☐ Eye Drops
☐ Credit/ATM Cards	☐ Reservation Docs/Tickets	☐ Travel Blanket/Pillow	☐
☐ Cash/Singles for Tips/Tolls	☐ Maps/Directions	☐ Food/Snacks	☐
☐ Insurance Cards	☐	☐ In-Flight Medication	
☐ Membership Cards (AAA, DVC)	☐	☐ Hand Sanitizer	

CARRY-ON

PACKING Checklist

TRAVELER	DESTINATION	DAYS	WEATHER

✓	QTY	TOPS	✓	QTY	BASICS	✓	OUTERWEAR/SWIMWEAR	✓	OTHER
		Dressy			Underwear		Swimsuits/Cover-up		
		Casual			Socks		Jacket/Sweatshirt		
		T-shirts			Bras/Undershirts		Hat		
		Exercise			Sleepwear				

QTY	BOTTOMS	QTY	ACCESSORIES	FOOTWEAR
	Dress Pants		Belts	Dress Shoes
	Jeans		Ties/Scarves	Athletic/Walking Shoes
	Shorts		Jewelry	Sandals/Flip-flops
	Exercise		Sunglasses	Water Shoes

CLOTHING

TOILETRIES

HYGIENE	HAIR CARE	COSMETICS	MISC.
☐ Toothbrush/Paste	☐ Shampoo/Conditioner	☐ Face Wash	☐ Tweezers
☐ Dental Floss/Mouthwash	☐ Comb/Brush	☐ Moisturizer	☐ Nail Clippers/File
☐ Contacts/Saline	☐ Styling Products	☐ Makeup	☐
☐ Deodorant	☐ Hairdryer	☐ Makeup Remover	☐
☐ Soap/Body Wash	☐ Curling/Flat Iron/Dryer	☐ Perfume	☐
☐ Feminine Products	☐ Hair Accessories	☐ Cotton Balls/Q-tips	☐
☐	☐	☐	☐

MISCELLANEOUS

HEALTH	GEAR	ELECTRONICS	MISC.
☐ Medication/Vitamins	☐ Laundry Bag	☐ Laptop/Tablet	☐ Ear Plugs
☐ Pain Relievers	☐ Pop Up Hamper	☐ iPod/e-Reader	☐ Clothespins/Safety Pins
☐ Anti-nausea Pills	☐ Backpack/Beach Tote	☐ Chargers/Batteries	☐ Flashlight
☐ First Aid Kit	☐ Collapsible Cooler	☐ Camera	☐ Small Scissors
☐ Sunscreen	☐ Collapsible Storage Bins	☐	☐

CARRY-ON

TRAVEL ID/FUNDS/DOCS	TRAVEL DOCUMENTS	TRAVEL AIDS	MISC.
Passport/Visa/ID	Itinerary	Ear Buds/Headphones	Eye Drops
Credit/ATM Cards	Reservation Docs/Tickets	Travel Blanket/Pillow	
Cash/Singles for Tips/Tolls	Maps/Directions	Food/Snacks	
Insurance Cards		In-Flight Medication	
Membership Cards (AAA, DVC)		Hand Sanitizer	

PACKING Checklist

TRAVELER	DESTINATION	DAYS	WEATHER

CLOTHING

✓	QTY	TOPS	✓	QTY	BASICS	✓	OUTERWEAR/SWIMWEAR	✓	OTHER
☐		Dressy	☐		Underwear	☐	Swimsuits/Cover-up	☐	
☐		Casual	☐		Socks	☐	Jacket/Sweatshirt	☐	
☐		T-shirts	☐		Bras/Undershirts	☐	Hat	☐	
☐		Exercise	☐		Sleepwear	☐		☐	
			☐					☐	

	QTY	BOTTOMS		QTY	ACCESSORIES		FOOTWEAR		
☐		Dress Pants	☐		Belts	☐	Dress Shoes		
☐		Jeans	☐		Ties/Scarves	☐	Athletic/Walking Shoes		
☐		Shorts	☐		Jewelry	☐	Sandals/Flip-flops		
☐		Exercise	☐		Sunglasses	☐	Water Shoes		

TOILETRIES

	HYGIENE		HAIR CARE		COSMETICS		MISC.
☐	Toothbrush/Paste	☐	Shampoo/Conditioner	☐	Face Wash	☐	Tweezers
☐	Dental Floss/Mouthwash	☐	Comb/Brush	☐	Moisturizer	☐	Nail Clippers/File
☐	Contacts/Saline	☐	Styling Products	☐	Makeup	☐	
☐	Deodorant	☐	Hairdryer	☐	Makeup Remover	☐	
☐	Soap/Body Wash	☐	Curling/Flat Iron/Dryer	☐	Perfume	☐	
☐	Feminine Products	☐	Hair Accessories	☐	Cotton Balls/Q-tips	☐	
☐		☐		☐		☐	

MISCELLANEOUS

	HEALTH		GEAR		ELECTRONICS		MISC.
☐	Medication/Vitamins	☐	Laundry Bag	☐	Laptop/Tablet	☐	Ear Plugs
☐	Pain Relievers	☐	Pop Up Hamper	☐	iPod/e-Reader	☐	Clothespins/Safety Pins
☐	Anti-nausea Pills	☐	Backpack/Beach Tote	☐	Chargers/Batteries	☐	Flashlight
☐	First Aid Kit	☐	Collapsible Cooler	☐	Camera	☐	Small Scissors
☐	Sunscreen	☐	Collapsible Storage Bins	☐		☐	

CARRY-ON

	TRAVEL ID/FUNDS/DOCS		TRAVEL DOCUMENTS		TRAVEL AIDS		MISC.
☐	Passport/Visa/ID	☐	Itinerary	☐	Ear Buds/Headphones	☐	Eye Drops
☐	Credit/ATM Cards	☐	Reservation Docs/Tickets	☐	Travel Blanket/Pillow		
☐	Cash/Singles for Tips/Tolls	☐	Maps/Directions	☐	Food/Snacks		
☐	Insurance Cards	☐		☐	In-Flight Medication		
☐	Membership Cards (AAA, DVC)	☐		☐	Hand Sanitizer		

PACKING Checklist

TRAVELER	DESTINATION	DAYS	WEATHER

PARK TOURING BAG

- ☐ Magic Bands/Tickets
- ☐ Drivers License/ID
- ☐ Cash/Credit Cards
- ☐ Membership Cards
- ☐ Dining Reservation #s
- ☐ Park Map
- ☐ Cell Phone
- ☐ Camera
- ☐ Chargers
- ☐ Lanyard

- ☐ Sunglasses
- ☐ Water bottles/Water
- ☐ Snacks
- ☐ Hand Towel
- ☐ Rain Poncho/Umbrella
- ☐ Hats/Visors
- ☐ Ziploc for Wet Clothes
- ☐ Dry Change of Clothes
- ☐
- ☐
- ☐

- ☐ Mini First Aid Kit
- ☐ Moleskin
- ☐ Pain Reliever
- ☐ Anti-Nausea Pills
- ☐ Sunscreen
- ☐ Insect Repellant
- ☐ Hand Sanitizer
- ☐ Wet Wipes
- ☐ Tissues
- ☐ Lip Balm

- ☐ Autograph Book/Pen
- ☐ Glow Sticks/Necklaces
- ☐ Pennies for Pressing
- ☐ Playing Cards/Games
- ☐ Bottles of Bubbles
- ☐ Pins for Trading
- ☐
- ☐
- ☐
- ☐

WATER PARK BAG

- ☐ Magic Bands/Tickets
- ☐ Drivers License/ID
- ☐ Cash/Credit Cards
- ☐ Waterproof Phone Case
- ☐ Camera
- ☐ Lanyard
- ☐ Sunglasses
- ☐ Water bottles/Water
- ☐ Snacks

- ☐ Bathing Suits
- ☐ Beach Towels
- ☐ Hats/Visors
- ☐ Beach Bag
- ☐ Dry Change of Clothes
- ☐ Ziploc for Wet Clothes
- ☐ Swim Diapers
- ☐ Water Shoes/Flip Flops
- ☐

- ☐ Mini First Aid Kit
- ☐ Ear Plugs
- ☐ Pain Reliever
- ☐ Anti-Nausea Pills
- ☐ Sunscreen /Lip Balm
- ☐ Insect Repellant
- ☐ Hand Sanitizer
- ☐ Wet Wipes
- ☐ Tissues

- ☐ Goggles
- ☐ Flotation Device
- ☐ Water Toys
- ☐ Books/Magazines
- ☐
- ☐
- ☐
- ☐

EVERYTHING BUT THE KITCHEN SINK!

- ☐
- ☐
- ☐
- ☐
- ☐
- ☐
- ☐
- ☐
- ☐
- ☐
- ☐

PACKING Checklist

	TRAVELER	DESTINATION	DAYS	WEATHER

PARK TOURING BAG

- [ ] Magic Bands/Tickets
- [ ] Drivers License/ID
- [ ] Cash/Credit Cards
- [ ] Membership Cards
- [ ] Dining Reservation #s
- [ ] Park Map
- [ ] Cell Phone
- [ ] Camera
- [ ] Chargers
- [ ] Lanyard
- [ ]

- [ ] Sunglasses
- [ ] Water bottles/Water
- [ ] Snacks
- [ ] Hand Towel
- [ ] Rain Poncho/Umbrella
- [ ] Hats/Visors
- [ ] Ziploc for Wet Clothes
- [ ] Dry Change of Clothes
- [ ]
- [ ]
- [ ]

- [ ] Mini First Aid Kit
- [ ] Moleskin
- [ ] Pain Reliever
- [ ] Anti-Nausea Pills
- [ ] Sunscreen
- [ ] Insect Repellant
- [ ] Hand Sanitizer
- [ ] Wet Wipes
- [ ] Tissues
- [ ] Lip Balm
- [ ]

- [ ] Autograph Book/Pen
- [ ] Glow Sticks/Necklaces
- [ ] Pennies for Pressing
- [ ] Playing Cards/Games
- [ ] Bottles of Bubbles
- [ ] Pins for Trading
- [ ]
- [ ]
- [ ]
- [ ]
- [ ]

WATER PARK BAG

- [ ] Magic Bands/Tickets
- [ ] Drivers License/ID
- [ ] Cash/Credit Cards
- [ ] Waterproof Phone Case
- [ ] Camera
- [ ] Lanyard
- [ ] Sunglasses
- [ ] Water bottles/Water
- [ ] Snacks

- [ ] Bathing Suits
- [ ] Beach Towels
- [ ] Hats/Visors
- [ ] Beach Bag
- [ ] Dry Change of Clothes
- [ ] Ziploc for Wet Clothes
- [ ] Swim Diapers
- [ ] Water Shoes/Flip Flops
- [ ]

- [ ] Mini First Aid Kit
- [ ] Ear Plugs
- [ ] Pain Reliever
- [ ] Anti-Nausea Pills
- [ ] Sunscreen /Lip Balm
- [ ] Insect Repellant
- [ ] Hand Sanitizer
- [ ] Wet Wipes
- [ ] Tissues

- [ ] Goggles
- [ ] Flotation Device
- [ ] Water Toys
- [ ] Books/Magazines
- [ ]
- [ ]
- [ ]
- [ ]
- [ ]

EVERYTHING BUT THE KITCHEN SINK!

☐	☐	☐	☐
☐	☐	☐	☐
☐	☐	☐	☐
☐	☐	☐	☐
☐	☐	☐	☐
☐	☐	☐	☐
☐	☐	☐	☐
☐	☐	☐	☐
☐	☐	☐	☐
☐	☐	☐	☐
☐	☐	☐	☐

PACKING Checklist

PARK TOURING BAG

- Magic Bands/Tickets
- Drivers License/ID
- Cash/Credit Cards
- Membership Cards
- Dining Reservation #s
- Park Map
- Cell Phone
- Camera
- Chargers
- Lanyard

- Sunglasses
- Water bottles/Water
- Snacks
- Hand Towel
- Rain Poncho/Umbrella
- Hats/Visors
- Ziploc for Wet Clothes
- Dry Change of Clothes

- Mini First Aid Kit
- Moleskin
- Pain Reliever
- Anti-Nausea Pills
- Sunscreen
- Insect Repellant
- Hand Sanitizer
- Wet Wipes
- Tissues
- Lip Balm

- Autograph Book/Pen
- Glow Sticks/Necklaces
- Pennies for Pressing
- Playing Cards/Games
- Bottles of Bubbles
- Pins for Trading

WATER PARK BAG

- Magic Bands/Tickets
- Drivers License/ID
- Cash/Credit Cards
- Waterproof Phone Case
- Camera
- Lanyard
- Sunglasses
- Water bottles/Water
- Snacks

- Bathing Suits
- Beach Towels
- Hats/Visors
- Beach Bag
- Dry Change of Clothes
- Ziploc for Wet Clothes
- Swim Diapers
- Water Shoes/Flip Flops

- Mini First Aid Kit
- Ear Plugs
- Pain Reliever
- Anti-Nausea Pills
- Sunscreen /Lip Balm
- Insect Repellant
- Hand Sanitizer
- Wet Wipes
- Tissues

- Goggles
- Flotation Device
- Water Toys
- Books/Magazines

EVERYTHING BUT THE KITCHEN SINK!

PACKING Checklist

TRAVELER	DESTINATION	DAYS	WEATHER

PARK TOURING BAG

- ☐ Magic Bands/Tickets
- ☐ Drivers License/ID
- ☐ Cash/Credit Cards
- ☐ Membership Cards
- ☐ Dining Reservation #s
- ☐ Park Map
- ☐ Cell Phone
- ☐ Camera
- ☐ Chargers
- ☐ Lanyard
- ☐

- ☐ Sunglasses
- ☐ Water bottles/Water
- ☐ Snacks
- ☐ Hand Towel
- ☐ Rain Poncho/Umbrella
- ☐ Hats/Visors
- ☐ Ziploc for Wet Clothes
- ☐ Dry Change of Clothes
- ☐
- ☐
- ☐

- ☐ Mini First Aid Kit
- ☐ Moleskin
- ☐ Pain Reliever
- ☐ Anti-Nausea Pills
- ☐ Sunscreen
- ☐ Insect Repellant
- ☐ Hand Sanitizer
- ☐ Wet Wipes
- ☐ Tissues
- ☐ Lip Balm
- ☐

- ☐ Autograph Book/Pen
- ☐ Glow Sticks/Necklaces
- ☐ Pennies for Pressing
- ☐ Playing Cards/Games
- ☐ Bottles of Bubbles
- ☐ Pins for Trading
- ☐
- ☐
- ☐
- ☐

WATER PARK BAG

- ☐ Magic Bands/Tickets
- ☐ Drivers License/ID
- ☐ Cash/Credit Cards
- ☐ Waterproof Phone Case
- ☐ Camera
- ☐ Lanyard
- ☐ Sunglasses
- ☐ Water bottles/Water
- ☐ Snacks

- ☐ Bathing Suits
- ☐ Beach Towels
- ☐ Hats/Visors
- ☐ Beach Bag
- ☐ Dry Change of Clothes
- ☐ Ziploc for Wet Clothes
- ☐ Swim Diapers
- ☐ Water Shoes/Flip Flops
- ☐

- ☐ Mini First Aid Kit
- ☐ Ear Plugs
- ☐ Pain Reliever
- ☐ Anti-Nausea Pills
- ☐ Sunscreen /Lip Balm
- ☐ Insect Repellant
- ☐ Hand Sanitizer
- ☐ Wet Wipes
- ☐ Tissues

- ☐ Goggles
- ☐ Flotation Device
- ☐ Water Toys
- ☐ Books/Magazines
- ☐
- ☐
- ☐
- ☐
- ☐

EVERYTHING BUT THE KITCHEN SINK!

☐	☐	☐	☐
☐	☐	☐	☐
☐	☐	☐	☐
☐	☐	☐	☐
☐	☐	☐	☐
☐	☐	☐	☐
☐	☐	☐	☐
☐	☐	☐	☐
☐	☐	☐	☐
☐	☐	☐	☐
☐	☐	☐	☐

PACKING Checklist

	TRAVELER	DESTINATION	DAYS	WEATHER
				☀ ☁ 🌧

PARK TOURING BAG

☐ Magic Bands/Tickets	☐ Sunglasses	☐ Mini First Aid Kit	☐ Autograph Book/Pen
☐ Drivers License/ID	☐ Water bottles/Water	☐ Moleskin	☐ Glow Sticks/Necklaces
☐ Cash/Credit Cards	☐ Snacks	☐ Pain Reliever	☐ Pennies for Pressing
☐ Membership Cards	☐ Hand Towel	☐ Anti-Nausea Pills	☐ Playing Cards/Games
☐ Dining Reservation #s	☐ Rain Poncho/Umbrella	☐ Sunscreen	☐ Bottles of Bubbles
☐ Park Map	☐ Hats/Visors	☐ Insect Repellant	☐ Pins for Trading
☐ Cell Phone	☐ Ziploc for Wet Clothes	☐ Hand Sanitizer	☐
☐ Camera	☐ Dry Change of Clothes	☐ Wet Wipes	☐
☐ Chargers	☐	☐ Tissues	☐
☐ Lanyard	☐	☐ Lip Balm	☐
☐	☐	☐	☐

WATER PARK BAG

☐ Magic Bands/Tickets	☐ Bathing Suits	☐ Mini First Aid Kit	☐ Goggles
☐ Drivers License/ID	☐ Beach Towels	☐ Ear Plugs	☐ Flotation Device
☐ Cash/Credit Cards	☐ Hats/Visors	☐ Pain Reliever	☐ Water Toys
☐ Waterproof Phone Case	☐ Beach Bag	☐ Anti-Nausea Pills	☐ Books/Magazines
☐ Camera	☐ Dry Change of Clothes	☐ Sunscreen /Lip Balm	☐
☐ Lanyard	☐ Ziploc for Wet Clothes	☐ Insect Repellant	☐
☐ Sunglasses	☐ Swim Diapers	☐ Hand Sanitizer	☐
☐ Water bottles/Water	☐ Water Shoes/Flip Flops	☐ Wet Wipes	☐
☐ Snacks	☐	☐ Tissues	☐

EVERYTHING BUT THE KITCHEN SINK!

☐	☐	☐	☐
☐	☐	☐	☐
☐	☐	☐	☐
☐	☐	☐	☐
☐	☐	☐	☐
☐	☐	☐	☐
☐	☐	☐	☐
☐	☐	☐	☐
☐	☐	☐	☐
☐	☐	☐	☐
☐	☐	☐	☐

PACKING Checklist

TRAVELER	DESTINATION	DAYS	WEATHER
			🌡 ° ☀ ⛅ 🌧

CLOTHING

☐	☐	☐
☐	☐	☐
☐	☐	☐
☐	☐	☐
☐	☐	☐
☐	☐	☐
☐	☐	☐
☐	☐	☐
☐	☐	☐
☐	☐	☐

TOILETRIES

☐	☐	☐
☐	☐	☐
☐	☐	☐
☐	☐	☐
☐	☐	☐
☐	☐	☐
☐	☐	☐

MISCELLANEOUS

☐	☐	☐
☐	☐	☐
☐	☐	☐
☐	☐	☐
☐	☐	☐
☐	☐	☐

CARRY-ON

☐	☐	☐
☐	☐	☐
☐	☐	☐
☐	☐	☐
☐	☐	☐
☐	☐	☐

PACKING Checklist

TRAVELER	DESTINATION	DAYS	WEATHER

CLOTHING

TOILETRIES

MISCELLANEOUS

CARRY-ON

PACKING Checklist

TRAVELER	DESTINATION	DAYS	WEATHER

CLOTHING

- [ ]   - [ ]   - [ ]
- [ ]   - [ ]   - [ ]
- [ ]   - [ ]   - [ ]
- [ ]   - [ ]   - [ ]
- [ ]   - [ ]   - [ ]
- [ ]   - [ ]   - [ ]
- [ ]   - [ ]   - [ ]
- [ ]   - [ ]   - [ ]
- [ ]   - [ ]   - [ ]
- [ ]   - [ ]   - [ ]
- [ ]   - [ ]   - [ ]

TOILETRIES

- [ ]   - [ ]   - [ ]
- [ ]   - [ ]   - [ ]
- [ ]   - [ ]   - [ ]
- [ ]   - [ ]   - [ ]
- [ ]   - [ ]   - [ ]
- [ ]   - [ ]   - [ ]
- [ ]   - [ ]   - [ ]

MISCELLANEOUS

- [ ]   - [ ]   - [ ]
- [ ]   - [ ]   - [ ]
- [ ]   - [ ]   - [ ]
- [ ]   - [ ]   - [ ]
- [ ]   - [ ]   - [ ]
- [ ]   - [ ]   - [ ]

CARRY-ON

- [ ]   - [ ]   - [ ]
- [ ]   - [ ]   - [ ]
- [ ]   - [ ]   - [ ]
- [ ]   - [ ]   - [ ]
- [ ]   - [ ]   - [ ]
- [ ]   - [ ]   - [ ]

PACKING Checklist

TRAVELER	DESTINATION	DAYS	WEATHER
			🌡 __° ☀ ⛅ 🌧

CLOTHING

- [ ]
- [ ]
- [ ]
- [ ]
- [ ]
- [ ]
- [ ]
- [ ]
- [ ]
- [ ]

TOILETRIES

- [ ]
- [ ]
- [ ]
- [ ]
- [ ]
- [ ]
- [ ]

MISCELLANEOUS

- [ ]
- [ ]
- [ ]
- [ ]
- [ ]
- [ ]

CARRY-ON

- [ ]
- [ ]
- [ ]
- [ ]
- [ ]
- [ ]

PACKING Checklist

TRAVELER	DESTINATION	DAYS	WEATHER
			° ☀ ⛅ 🌧

CLOTHING

- ☐
- ☐
- ☐
- ☐
- ☐
- ☐
- ☐
- ☐
- ☐
- ☐

TOILETRIES

- ☐
- ☐
- ☐
- ☐
- ☐
- ☐
- ☐

MISCELLANEOUS

- ☐
- ☐
- ☐
- ☐
- ☐
- ☐

CARRY-ON

- ☐
- ☐
- ☐
- ☐
- ☐
- ☐

SHOPPING List

CLOTHING

TOILETRIES

MISCELLANEOUS

CARRY-ON

SHOPPING List

CLOTHING

TOILETRIES

MISCELLANEOUS

CARRY-ON

SHOPPING List

CLOTHING

TOILETRIES

- [ ]
- [ ]
- [ ]
- [ ]
- [ ]
- [ ]
- [ ]
- [ ]

- [ ]
- [ ]
- [ ]
- [ ]
- [ ]
- [ ]
- [ ]
- [ ]

- [ ]
- [ ]
- [ ]
- [ ]
- [ ]
- [ ]
- [ ]
- [ ]

MISCELLANEOUS

- [ ]
- [ ]
- [ ]
- [ ]
- [ ]
- [ ]

- [ ]
- [ ]
- [ ]
- [ ]
- [ ]
- [ ]

- [ ]
- [ ]
- [ ]
- [ ]
- [ ]
- [ ]

CARRY-ON

- [ ]
- [ ]
- [ ]
- [ ]
- [ ]

- [ ]
- [ ]
- [ ]
- [ ]
- [ ]

- [ ]
- [ ]
- [ ]
- [ ]
- [ ]

SHOPPING List

CLOTHING

TOILETRIES

MISCELLANEOUS

CARRY-ON

SHOPPING List

CLOTHING

TOILETRIES

MISCELLANEOUS

CARRY-ON

NOTES

NOTES

NOTES

NOTES

NOTES

NOTES